How to Simplify Your LOE

A Guide to a Happier, More Fulfilling Relationship

Marion Küstenmacher
Werner Tiki Küstenmacher
Bestselling Author of *How to Simplify Your Life*

McGraw Hill

New York   Chicago   San Francisco   Lisbon   London   Madrid   Mexico City
Milan   New Delhi   San Juan   Seoul   Singapore   Sydney   Toronto

Library of Congress Cataloging-in-Publication Data

Küstenmacher, Marion.
    How to simplify your love : a guide to a happier, more fulfilling relationship / Marion and Werner Tiki Küstenmacher ; translated by Jennifer Cameron.
        p.   cm.
    ISBN-13: 978-0-07-149917-0 (alk. paper)
    ISBN-10: 0-07-149917-2 (alk. paper)
    1. Love.   2. Interpersonal relations.   I. Küstenmacher, Werner.   II. Title.

BF575.L8K88   2008
152.4′1—dc22   2008009856

1 2 3 4 5 6 7 8 9 10 11 12 13 14 15 16 17 18 19 20 21 22 23 24 25   FGR/FGR   0 9 8

ISBN   978-0-07-149917-0
MHID   0-07-149917-2

McGraw-Hill books are available at special quantity discounts to use as premiums and sales promotions or for use in corporate training programs. To contact a representative, please visit the Contact Us pages at www.mhprofessional.com.

This book is printed on acid-free paper.

Contents

Contents

Preface

The Floating Heart

When the two of us took over editing the advice column "Simplify Your Life" in 1998 and set up a telephone hotline, it wasn't long before we realized which topic took first place on the list of life's complications: the relationship question. Nowhere was there more bewilderment and desperation; nowhere was so much confusion and feelings of entitlement endured. A chaotic household or an office buried under paperwork was nothing compared to the complicated nature of relationships. Nothing demanded simplification as much as the vast issue of love between men and women. Although we aren't counselors for couples therapy, throughout all these years we have tried to bring a bit of order to relationships through our articles and to build bridges between "me" and "you."

The two of us came to this subject in different ways:

Years of leading self-development seminars have helped Marion to understand relationships from a systematic, process-oriented perspective. This experience allowed her to develop our model of the five dwellings of love. Many of the practical insights  in this book come from the conversations of participants in these seminars, and we sincerely thank them.

Since his book *How to Simplify Your Life* (2001), Tiki has given many talks, signed books afterward, and drawn a little picture in nearly every copy. The most commonly requested motif was an illustration that he usually showed at the end of his presentation. He hasn't kept an exact count, but he has probably drawn this picture nearly a thousand times. Many people have sent in photos of the picture hanging over the sofa in their living room; it has become a popular theme for wedding sermons and a kind of modern coat-of-arms on business cards. The overwhelming resonance of this simple little drawing was what eventually encouraged us to write a book about love. From this, we once again have learned how much emotional support can be gained from a positive image: progress requires imagination, and images inspire progress.

Two People on Two Islands

The picture is a symbol of a modern partnership, and it shows two islands, a man on one and a woman on the other. These two people actually belong together, yet they live in two separate worlds: he in his world and she in hers. It is an image of longing: how we wish to find a partner! It is also an illustration of how we merge into each other and become one, forgetting ourselves and moving onto a shared island, however small it may be.

But there are no such small, lone islands for two, and there probably never were. The romantic fantasy of complete unity has one crucial catch for modern individuals: even if they become a couple, each lover retains his or her unique identity. Each still has his or her very own feelings and identities, entirely personal history, individual dreams and longings, own personality type, and unique strengths and weaknesses. Each may ask: "Who am I? Where do I belong?" You don't have to forget yourself and give yourself to someone else anymore. Does that mean, though, that we should just forget the whole love thing? That two people will never really belong together?

When this question comes up, Tiki draws the rest of the picture: the two islands actually are the peaks of a giant heart-shaped floating island. Just like an iceberg, 90 percent of this island lies beneath the surface. This is not only a clever illustrative device, but also a scientifically proven, psychological fact: a couple shares a common unconscious that holds them together.

What Happened Before This Picture

As you were floating alone through the sea of life, your self was a relatively small sheet of ice. It was just the right size for you alone. But then when you found your partner, something wonderful happened: your self deepened. As the psychologists say, your specific weight increased.

Since you found each other, you have grown inside and gained depth, stability, and security. You've sailed into calmer waters. A new energy flowed through you, an energy that didn't come from within you. Did it come from your beloved?

If you look closely, you will see that the same thing has happened to your partner. The energy that he or she is experiencing didn't come from you or from inside your partner. The energy is greater than the two of you. Something happened that was stronger than both of your lives together, than both of your feelings, and than your shared experiences and dreams.

Throughout all of the arguments and turbulence that you experience, something is holding you together. You are supported by something beneath you, which you can rely upon. Many people don't realize this until they want to separate. They live in murky water and see only all of the problems that come between them: "We don't have anything to say to each other anymore," "We've grown apart from each other," or "We aren't really a couple, just two people living next to each other," like the two tracks of a railroad that meet only at infinity, as the writer Paulo Coelho once described it. Then they are amazed at how painful and wearying it is to try to separate. It is exhausting and nearly impossible to take and simply destroy these powerful, stable bonds, which often have had many years to grow.

Two Common Misconceptions

We see it again and again: people *over*estimate what lies *above* the waterline and *under*estimate what holds them up *beneath* the surface of their lives. What they consciously see are the compatibilities up above the surface of the two islands: the everyday agreements in taste and preferences, and in their intuitive and practical togetherness. But they underestimate the compatibilities in their souls, which have merged deep beneath them into a supporting force.

This is the fundamental simplifying tip of this book: rely upon love. It can support you. Relax. Your life is not as superficial as it sometimes seems. There is something beneath the surface that is greater than you. So *How to Simplify Your Love* is actually nothing more than a course in developing trust and calmness.

The love that you have experienced, whether tumultuous or peaceful, whether with powerful squalls or gradual, gentle swells—the two of you didn't invent this love (even if it sometimes seems like you are the first two people in the world to have felt something like this). This love is the great power of life, primal and yet always new, the secret of the human heart. You have this power to thank for your own birth, for having fallen in love, and for having stayed together.

Why It's So Difficult Today

Although we are in no way nostalgic, we do sometimes think that couples in past generations may actually have had it easier. The "marriage ship" was already there for them; they didn't have to invent it. In those days, you could embark on the ship called *Marriage* that was ready and waiting for you. You went ceremoniously on board under a shower of applause and sailed along proudly in a stately fleet of similar ships.

Today, however, most couples board this love boat with heavy baggage. They have to ask themselves the questions: "Do we want to marry at all?" and "Why?" Popular magazines bombard them with the seemingly scientific findings that humans are not at all suited for monogamy. They read frustrating statistics about the likelihood of their partnership ending in divorce. When yet another relationship falls apart in their circle of friends, they accept it as inevitable. They don't have any other image in their hearts from which they can draw strength and confidence.

But the image of the floating heart in the sea of life is just such an image, and it's there for you whenever you wonder, "Where is love?" It reassures you that this floating island of love is stronger than it seems. It will be there even if one of you goes overboard, loses his or her way, and confusedly seeks out other islands. Even some couples who have been together for years admit to having almost split up, but then found each other once again. And when one person falls overboard, it isn't always his or her own fault. Life is full of storms that can really threaten your togetherness. But storms don't capsize an island, and you have many chances to scramble back on land.

A Space of Your Own

The image of the floating heart bears one more encouraging message: that little island you're sitting on belongs to you. On the big heart you share, each of you has your own place that the other can't take away from you. You can settle your island with plants and buildings, making yourself at home on your half of the heart. That's how you show that you are filling this partnership with life and shaping it lovingly. Your area is your own; it corresponds to your way of loving and of being yourself. Many people ask themselves, "Where am I?" when they don't make themselves comfortable on the island of their partnership. Our picture should offer you the confidence to create your own space on the island, supported by the wonder-ful power of love. You will even find that you have more room for yourself than you ever had by yourself on your little sheet of ice.

Take to heart the image of the floating heart. The underlying message of *How to Simplify Your Love* is that love can support you. Keep that in mind as you begin the journey of getting to know the five dwellings of love.

We'll start with a dream . . .

Acknowledgments

Our book couldn't have been written without the cooperation of many people—and above all, not without the engagement of everyone who, together with us, forms the great community of the *Simplify* Company. Our heartfelt thanks go out to:

Detlef Koenig, publisher of our monthly advice newsletter in the VNR Verlag für die Deutsche Wirtschaft AG (VNR Publisher for the German Economy) and inexhaustible engine of the *Simplify Your Life®* brand. The *Simplify* concept owes its market success to his professionalism and organizational ability. We know what we've got in you!

Thomas Carl Schwoerer, publisher of our *Simplify* books at Campus, who together with his highly motivated team saw to it that we had freedom of thought, critical camaraderie, and a vision of the future in book form. How wonderful to have you as part of the German cultural landscape!

Christiane Meyer, a dream of an editor, who coached us kindly, intelligently, and with the patience of an angel right up to the submission deadline. You have earned the *Simplify* medal!

Constanze Keutler and Silke Thinschmidt, our editorial assistants, who have researched with a love for detail, spurred us on, and as critical first readers, tested the book for its everyday suitability.

Acknowledgments

Dorothea Zimmer, psychologist at FreshConnections—integral, who gave us valuable insights into Spiral Dynamics—integral.

Charlotte and Heinz Küstenmacher, Oskar and Roswitha Ruck-däschel, our parents. As couples in difficult times as these, you have founded a family and stood by each other in good days and bad. The great river of love flows on in memory of you.

Introduction

Welcome to the Land of Love

You dream of an unknown hand being placed on your shoulder. It is gentle and loving, but at the same time it has an enormous strength that effortlessly lifts you up. You are floating over a landscape at dawn. You look down, and you know that this vast region extending out to the horizon and far beyond it is all your land. The life you have lived and have yet to live stretches out beneath you. It's astonishingly huge, a whole continent covered by a delicate blue mist. You can hardly orient yourself, but you love this land from deep within your heart. You wonder at that, but only for a short moment, because it then occurs to you what this immeasurably vast and wonderful land beneath you is: it's called love.

Love, the Dark Continent

That's what author Ingeborg Bachmann called this land, which no one knows and everyone longs for. Draped in a fine mist, it waits to be discovered. With this book, we want to help you explore this magnificent continent and better understand its secrets. If you're single, you will

discover that your piece of the land of love isn't as small as you thought. If you're already in a relationship, you will notice that you can rediscover and conquer immense parts of it—without having to find a new partner.

The two of us have been together since 1977 and have been married since 1980. Throughout our long years in the kingdom of partnership and love, we, like countless other couples, have learned that life as a couple is not a fixed, predetermined state. We don't just settle down forever in the land of love. We and our partner constantly change. Anyone who enters into a partnership undertakes a great journey where one encounters oneself and one's partner in ever new ways. Love is a shared adventure, described with splendid images in countless myths: a quest, a grand voyage. The grand journey of each couple is unique and unmistakable, just as no person is quite like another. There are, however, five typical stations or residences that a couple visits during their journey. These we have called the five dwellings of love.

Who This Book Is Written For

On the one hand, this book is intended for single people who want to prepare for a relationship. If you are single, it helps you familiarize yourself with the kingdom of love before you begin a relationship. It's like reading a guidebook before setting out on that trip you've always wanted to take. In reading this book, you will dream, plan, anticipate, and prepare yourself for the journey ahead.

On the other hand, *How to Simplify Your Love* is a book for couples of all ages. We would like to show you the great potential of your relationship. If you would like to know more about where you are in your relationship, to understand each other better, and to deepen your love for each other, this book is also for you.

Let us take you by the hand and set off on a journey into the inner world of your relationship. Orient yourself: which dwelling of love are you living in right now? Which do you have behind you and which ones lie before you still? Many couples won't occupy all five dwellings, but they'll still have a deep relationship with each other. Precisely at that moment, it can be important for you to reflect together about why you can't or don't want to visit an important station in the land of love.

The Five Dwellings of Love

We would actually prefer not to give away all of the stages right at the start, because the book would be more exciting to read if you didn't know them all. But before your curiosity makes you read ahead, here is an overview of the five dwellings of your love:

The tower
The love tent
The homestead
The dark forest
The castle

The journey always begins in the *tower*. The tower stands for you yourself as a unique individual. We're thinking of your healthy strength as an individual, your self-esteem, and your development. This building even has a secret room!

The *love tent* is a magical place that all people in love long for. In this wonderfully simple, improvised shelter, the lovers find each other, give themselves over to love, and forget the world around them.

Later, the couple moves into the *homestead*. This is the place where the two lovers adjust to one another, where everyday life, career, and family claim a large part of their energy and where they must hold on to their love through the pressures of everyday life.

Bordering all of these dwellings is the *dark forest*, in which one person or the other can sometimes lose his or her way. This deep forest stands for the difficult times, for all the crises and catastrophes that arise in the partnership.

At the end of the path, the entrance to the *royal castle* beckons. This is the magnificent promise for every couple. The tent is not the ultimate experience of love. The stress of the homestead does not last forever. The dark forest doesn't have to mean the end. As a couple, you can discover your castle beyond all of those other dwellings and arrive in a new dimension of love, maturity, and personal integrity. The castle, rising far above the landscape with a fantastic panoramic view, symbolizes the most encompassing aspect of your love, which stretches far beyond you and your family. It extends out into the community, benefits the whole country, reaches out into the universe, and can even continue beyond the limits of your own lifetime.

A Landscape Without Highways

There are no paved roads through the land of love. You and your partner create your own paths, alone and together.

There are also no highways in the land of love, just as there is no patented formula for a couple's happiness: your marital vows are no guarantee that your relationship will last so that you'll be able to spend your whole life happily ever after in the land of love. Consciously choosing *not* to marry doesn't ensure the relationship either. Similarly, children are as little a recipe for eternal bonding as is planned childlessness, where the two people in love can concentrate on

each other with no distractions. Everyone can reach the castle, those with kids and without, married and divorced, poor and rich, healthy and ill. There are only two traits that prevent people from entering the royal castle: indifference and ignorance.

Become Diligent and Clever in Love

Perhaps the greatest relationship killer is indifference. The success of your partnership depends on your dedication. That means dedication on each person's part. Invest your time, love, and effort into your relationship. Remember that you create your own love—you aren't at the mercy of it. Work at your relationship, even if it seems your partner doesn't. Continue to foster your relationship, without judging your partner's contributions. You don't want to become the demanding micromanager who suffocates his or her partner.

The other main cause for the failure of love is, unfortunately, ignorance, a lack of understanding of matters of the heart. Your body has a natural desire to be with a partner, thanks to your hormones and your sexuality. For the more emotional aspects of your relationship, however, you will need your brain, your imagination, your understanding, your heart, and your spiritual drive. Anyone who claims that he or she can succeed in a love relationship without continuing the process of self-discovery and exploration has bleak prospects. That person will probably find that his or her love eventually freezes up or dries out.

The good news, though, is that that's not going to happen to you. If you keep reading this book and exploring the land of love, then you have nothing to fear.

What We Believe

Many couples separate because one person says, "This relationship is holding me back." We believe, however, that a person can't discover his or her deepest and inmost possibilities alone. A person will always need to see him- or herself reflected in some You. We believe that love is the greatest shared opportunity for growth between a man and a woman. We believe this is possible for everyone, whether you are in a relationship or not. We believe in the powerful feelings that await you in the kingdom of love. We also believe, however, that many couples don't realize all that awaits them in the great, unknown empire of love. As we've said before, this book is like a helpful guidebook. It doesn't replace the tour itself, but it can help you avoid a wrong turn or keep you from losing your way altogether.

But enough explanation—let us now begin our journey!

The First Dwelling of Love
The Tower

Your Simplifying Dream: The Tower

As you slowly drift downward, you are still gazing, lost in thought, at the landscape before your eyes. You touch down gently, grateful to feel the solid ground under your feet. A delicate fog surrounds you. You see a light in front of and up above you. A mighty tower looms before you. Completely solitary, it rises from the landscape like a pillar. It is beautiful and strangely familiar, as if you had been there many times before.

Light comes from a small window set high in the facade. Something wonderful is shining there, gentle and friendly. As you walk around the tower, you find an open door. You go inside, where a broad, winding staircase greets you. Each step, each stone is familiar. Scents that you remember from your childhood waft to your nose. Countless memories come forth as you slowly climb the stairs. The first are from your youth, followed gradually by images from your adult years. A bit farther up is a windowless landing with a hearth, where a cozy wood fire crackles. An armchair invites you to sit down in front of the fire. You look into the flames and reflect upon the mysterious room whose warm light you saw shimmering from outside. It must lie somewhere above you, and there must be an entrance. You need to get in there, so you stand up to continue searching for it.

At the beginning of the journey toward love stands a single tower. Before there are two people who love each other, there is one person who longs to love and to be loved. Without requited love, most people feel lonely. This is why the tower stands alone at first. Whether you are a man or a woman, this tower is the perspective from which you view the entire world—it represents yourself and your lifelong process of becoming yourself. Your tower is the basis of your existence, and it remains your personal point of reference for your entire life. When you say "I," you speak from your tower.

Simplifying Idea 1: Get to Know Yourself

When a tower appears in a fairy tale, it usually represents the ego-center or the identity of an individual. We have chosen this symbol deliberately: your self is no primitive cave, no modest cottage, no ritzy palace, but rather a distinctly formed and clearly visible, upright structure. In this landscape the tower doesn't stand in a bustling, populated place, but in an unpopulated area. Your tower stands out distinctly from its surroundings. This means that you, as an adult, should be able to stand up for yourself and support yourself alone. As we are growing up, we are actually building our own freestanding tower. This tower should not stand too close to our parents' towers, nor should it lean on them. This often is not so simple, and it requires bravery, strength, and dedication. A tower can become crooked or even come crashing down when it has been built carelessly or exorbitantly high. Most important, however, even the most beautiful tower is not a true home, no matter how much security and protection it offers.

The tower metaphor may seem to imply that those living inside look out of the window and long to be somewhere else. However, some people choose to remain alone in their towers for life, either because they prefer to be alone or because they have not made it very far in the land of love.

From a psychological perspective, the stable tower is your symbol for a well-developed personality. It represents the core of your person and the source of your emotions. If you have access to this center, you feel a calming reserve inside yourself: you trust yourself and know who you are. You should feel good about your tower! It's exciting to spend a life exploring your own tower and discovering all that it contains. This is especially important if you want to form a lasting partnership with another person. After all, your partner has a tower of his or her own and is having similar experiences.

Have the Courage to Become an Individual

To understand how two towers relate to one another, it helps to distinguish between a *collectively oriented* personality and an *individually oriented* personality. Having a collectively oriented personality means that you are strongly determined by your unconscious and by society, and you are therefore cut off from yourself. You do what you are supposed to do, and it's important to you what others think of you. You go to a movie because everyone "has" to have seen it, you wear certain clothes because they are "must-haves" in your social circle, you buy a fancy car because one "has" to have one in your position, and so on.

If, however, you learn to relate truthfully to yourself and to others, you become an individually oriented personality. You then apply all of your resources toward becoming a genuine personality and give your tower its own facade. Your construction will be unmistakable with paths, openings, passages, windows, and guest rooms in just the right places, exactly where you want them to be.

If the collective is overemphasized, you end up alienated from yourself: you have a tower that fits in perfectly with popular attitudes, but you can't get rid of the terrible feeling that it's no good or that it's hollow inside. But if you are an individual, your sense of self is strengthened and lifted to a higher dimension. Don't let yourself be led astray by voices that criticize individualism as antisocial. Only when you dare to climb your own winding staircase and set upon your individual path of development will you begin to have the inner strength to love another person from the bottom of your heart! Only two *individuals* can dare to encounter themselves in love, to open themselves to each other, and to find their way together.

Well into the twentieth century, people thought that a good couple required only the man to have a fixed identity, a finished tower. The woman either didn't need to develop her own tower identity at all or she was to give it up as quickly as possible after marriage, adjust herself to her husband's identity, and concentrate completely on supporting him. In our society, we thankfully have moved past this way of thinking, and no one would want to turn the clock back. Women as well as men have the right to feel valuable and irreplaceable. Today, no one manages to achieve happiness through total self-sacrifice living in the shadow of another.

In practical terms, this means that the best prerequisite for a good relationship is two stable, freestanding towers. If you are permanently weak and in need of support, or if you think that your partner should always smooth out all of your weaknesses, then you and your partner are not a balanced match. In that case, you should have the courage to fully develop your own individuality and seek out a partner who is an individual as well.

The Outer Walls: Your Ego

A good tower requires sturdy walls. Your self-awareness is strong when your tower has a deep foundation and well-executed stonework. Then it can stand on its own. Insecure people who strongly rely on their parents, external authorities, or a partner find that their walls begin to falter as soon as these supports are taken away.

The many stones in the outer walls of the tower form the more egocentric part of your personality. They comprise your ideas, value system, wishes, and needs—in short, the *ego*. The ego is not a bad thing. It functions as your bodyguard and offers you protection and grounding. With its help you can mark off your own borders and define yourself. Because it tells you what you like and don't like, the ego also gets involved in your choice of a partner. Do you have a set idea of how your dream man or woman should look (e.g., long hair, blue eyes, a certain arch to the eyebrows)? Those are the ego's preferences and desires. Your ego wants to shape, determine, and take control. It is a bit like an impertinent child, always wanting to have its way. Unfortunately, the more compliant you are with it, the more you give in to it, the more stubborn and demanding your ego tends to become—just like a child who is used to getting every wish.

If you always let your ego lead, you become more egocentric, rigid, stubborn—and harder to like. Your tower loses vitality, flexibility, receptivity, and empathy. Your walls form an insurmountable layer of defense. When the ego always has its way, not only does it shut you off from the outside world, but in the end, it also makes sure your tower mutates into a self-styled prison, completely isolating you from everyone else. When this happens, a partnership becomes impossible.

The Treasure Chamber: Your Spirit

Prospects would be bleak if there weren't something else inside of you. The true secret of your tower lies well hidden inside. Within the strong walls, a winding staircase leads up to a wonderful room: the mysterious treasure chamber. There the true essence of your life resides, well hidden and protected. It is the true center of your identity, your true self—your spirit.

As the real essence of your tower, your spirit should play a strong role in your life. When you are guided by the gentle yet mighty power of your spirit, you gain self-awareness and self-confidence. In a wonderful way you gain access to the power for good that lies undiscovered within you. The noble spirit is not proud or controlling like the ego; on the contrary, it longs to devote itself to another person and give itself away. It has the fantastic ability to connect to everything with creative love. And it has a transforming power. In 1 Corinthians 13:4–8 in the Bible, the apostle Paul described this in his famous song of praise to love: "Love is patient, love is kind. It does not envy, it does not boast, it is not proud. It is not rude, it is not self-seeking, it is not easily angered, it keeps no record of wrongs . . . it always protects, always trusts, always hopes, always perseveres." This does not describe an unrealistic utopia, but rather shows the primal strength of the spirit. Love is its element; the spirit is created to love. It would be terrible for your spirit to remain locked up inside the tower of your ego. You can rely on it: your spirit has a gift for entering whole-heartedly into love—regardless of whether it's love for a person or for God.

The Windows: Your Face to the World

When you feel true love for another person, you love him or her with the strength of your external personality as well as with the inner power of your spirit. Love is always a mixture of ego and spirit, the power of Me and the commitment to others. But for a reliable, long-lasting, and deep partnership, your spirit, not your ego, should set the tone. So if you want to develop a true ability to love, you need to discover your center and search for the mysterious room in the tower of your self to find your true spirit.

When you have finally found the hidden entrance to this treasure chamber, most likely you will stand there amazed awhile. Then, however, you must open the window of your tower room to let in the light of consciousness, so that your spirit can look out and shine into the world. Once you are brave enough to do this, you will notice something fascinating: people gravitate toward you, because your loving spirit makes you attractive to others. The French word for *magnet* is *l'aimant*, "that which loves," because it attracts and unifies. The spirit also works like an attractor or magnet, drawing other people to you. The French mystic Franz von Sales described this in the following way: with its love the spirit creates an "energy field of rapture," which no one can escape.

Please don't think, "That sounds good, but I can't do it." Don't say, "I'm too old, too simple, too busy, or not faithful enough for that." Those are the negative whisperings of your ego, and you can't let them discourage you. The spirit can awaken in every person at any time. It's never too late. The great Swiss psychologist C. G. Jung emphasized over and over that most people never really comprehend the creative possibilities of adulthood, because they think too one-sidedly of childhood when they hear the word *development*. Even adults can mature, learn, and change when they trust the direction of their spirit and learn to reduce the dominance of their ego.

Simplifying Idea 2: Get Closer to Yourself

On the inside of your tower is a staircase with large, flat steps. Imagine that there's a good hundred steps, each representing a year of your life. You have already climbed up a large part of the way. About every seven years, great changes take place in everyone's personality. The first three phases, from steps 1 through 21, are marked by socially established events: You started school when you were almost seven years old. At thirteen you officially became a teenager, and around thirteen to fourteen you were confirmed or took part in some other coming-of-age ceremony. You remained a legal minor until you were twenty-one.

Certainly a case can be made for extending the seven-year rhythm far beyond this. The psychoanalyst Clarissa Estés has researched and named the next twelve stages. No stage is better or more worthwhile than another; each has its own significance and can bring fulfillment.

Get to Know the Winding Staircase of Your Personal Growth

Confusion in a partnership often arises because one person doesn't recognize what stage of development he or she is currently in. Sometimes, you will find one stage very stressful, but another phase will feel like a relief to you. Treat all phases as meaningful steps on the path toward the full unfolding of your true spirit, to whose room in the tower the great winding staircase leads. Massive identity crises can be a part of this unfolding. These are actually growth spurts in your personal development.

Your inner path on the winding staircase in the tower always has one goal: it leads you to the true core of your identity. With every step you take, you allow the light of your good essential core to shine clearer through your tower and you allow for your personality to unfold. Your unique personality determines your pace through these phases. A forty-year-old can already be in the Realm of the Mist (years 77–84), while a seventy-year-old can still be stuck in the Age of Crises (years 35–42). Think of the seven-year rhythm as an approximation.

Your Full Lifetime: 15 Times 7 Years

- *Years 0–7: The time of physicality.* This is a time of intensive learning about the body: running, speaking, social contacts. In play, you test out your first concepts of partnership.
- *Years 7–14: The time of differentiation.* You develop your rational understanding. Your powers of imagination and self-awareness grow, and you form individual value systems.
- *Years 14–21: The time of physical completion.* Your sexuality awakens and develops. Your appearance and your image play a great role, as do cliques and friends. You reach maturity physically, while psychically you wrestle with insecurities and self-consciousness.
- *Years 21–28: The time of departure.* You strive for more autonomy and finally disengage from your parents. You discover new worlds of knowledge, career, and partnership. Your self-confidence becomes stronger.
- *Years 28–35: The time of parenthood.* This is a phase of work and achievement, where you can test your own values and concepts. You take care of your children and manage work projects and social

responsibilities. The care of godchildren or older dependents may gradually begin during this time as well.

■ *Years 36–42: The time of crises.* The beginning of your increased spiritual growth comes with irritations, changes, and inner as well as outer struggles, including ones that occur in your partnership. Depth, authenticity, and truth are the beckoning rewards for these struggles.

   ■ *Years 42–49: The time of the first spiritual wisdom.* You reflect on the past more clearly than before, but you are still aware of your limits. You gain vision and unlock new reserves of inner strength—often through a difficult period in your health, career, or private life.

■ *Years 49–56: The time of the underworld.* Your spirit is confronted with dark times. Your insights about yourself grow, while your partner may at times seem very far away. At the end of this shadowy time is a comprehensive initiation into the spiritual realm—this applies not just to the individual, but to the couple, too, who have stayed together through difficult times.

■ *Years 56–63: The time of decision.* You figure out which area of your life is your top priority and let go of nonessentials. These new insights determine the direction of your future endeavors. Your partner discovers surprising new aspects in you: concentrated energy and an understanding of what is really important.

■ *Years 63–70: The time of observation.* The knot unravels. A look down from the tower of mindfulness can cause you to reevaluate everything you've learned and integrate contradictions you've come across. You and your partner discover newfound gratitude and mutual acceptance.

■ *Years 70–77: The time of rejuvenation.* This may sound counterintuitive, considering your waning physical strength, but your inner wisdom gains resilience and flexibility as you gracefully relinquish the "objects of youth." In a broader sense, you let go and become even freer.

■ *Years 77–84: The time of the mist.* With humility, you gain intuitive knowledge of how to find greatness in the smallest things. Your perspective on the broader picture, trained through many years and trials, encompasses the future as well as the past.

■ *Years 84–91: The time of the weavers.* You understand the web of life and learn to interpret it. Others are drawn to your wisdom, and your advice becomes precious.

■ *Years 91–98: The time of subtlety.* You "glow from within" and are at peace with yourself. You feel the need to say less, and you can more and more simply "be."

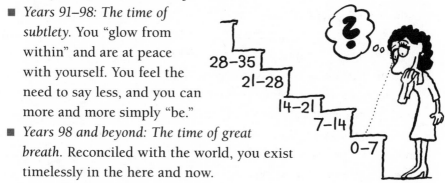

■ *Years 98 and beyond: The time of great breath.* Reconciled with the world, you exist timelessly in the here and now.

Make a note just for yourself—confidential and for your eyes only—of the most important moments of your life so far. Write down every event that occurs to you in the order that they come to mind—without putting pressure on yourself. Whatever occurs to you first is usually the event that has influenced you the most. This could be an illness, a death, an exceptionally happy experience, or even an unforgettable dream.

Find the Gift

Look over what you've written, and see if there is an inner logic to the order of your most important moments. Do you repeat certain patterns? Make a note under each event that you have gained something useful from to inform your life. You can find something valuable in even the difficult and tragic experiences! Ask your spirit what it has

 to say about these trying events. It will help you discover the hidden gift underneath the more difficult times. This gift counts above all and will enrich your partnership, because in the most influential moments of your life you learned to trust your inner strength.

Simplifying Idea 3: Fix Yourself Up

When people hear about the personality tower for the first time, they sometimes react dismissively, "I'm supposed to be a building? So alone and secluded, so stodgy and stony?" Then we tell them that their tower can be remodeled, just like every other building. You can work on your personality, clean out your tower in the same sense as the life pyramid in our book *How to Simplify Your Life*: make it nicer, homier, grander and friendlier! If you have just ended a relationship, this is good news for you. It means that you don't have to carry the hurt of your old relationships with you into the next one. With some relatively simple measures, you can become happier and thus also more attractive to others.

Make Friends with Yourself

Your first task in the land of love is to get to know your own tower so you can distinguish between your ego and your true self. Please don't misunderstand this to mean that your ego is bad and your self is intrinsically good (i.e., in the way that the word egotism has a negative connotation). Only when the two are united in harmony will they shine a warm light into the darkest corners of your tower. It's not about tearing yourself apart, but rather about something much happier: your ego and your self should be joined together. This heals your inner rifts and helps you achieve wholeness.

The Greek philosopher Aristotle calls this "friendship with oneself." Don't ask, "Who am I?" That question is typical of your lonely ego. Rather, your healthy, relationship-focused spirit wants to know,

"Who are we?" The spirit always has an eye for large, complex connections. Your spirit knows there are different aspects within you, some of which may be at odds with each other sometimes.

Who is this I? The sleepy guy who just woke up? The cheerful person who takes walks in the sunshine in the morning? The compassionate listener whom oth-ers come to when they need a shoulder to cry on? That little pile of misery who can feel so infinitely alone in the evenings? Is your I that feeling in your stomach? That feeling in your heart, sometimes a pang, sometimes a warmth? Your self-esteem and self-doubt? Yes, and there are even the different obstinate thoughts within your head and the contradictory feelings in your stomach. Each of these parts is an I of its own. Bringing all these parts together so that they form a We is how to make friends with yourself. You have numerous opportunities to practice this.

Being Yourself. The best starting point is your own body. You experience well-being and pain, you are healthy and sick, and sometimes you feel comfortable in your skin, sometimes decidedly uncomfortable. The first lesson is that these opposites are good and right—they make you feel alive! You can't feel the value of health without sickness. You only feel good when you are attentive and kind to your body. Learn to see your body as more than just a machine that needs to be repaired or "balanced" with medication. Your body is a highly sensitive seismograph that constantly provides you subtle bits of information about how you are really doing, what does you good and what doesn't. Train yourself to accurately perceive your bodily sensations now in your tower; then in a relationship these same inner antennae will be attuned to your partner's body, not your own, and later possibly to your children's.

Self-Realization. Your ego is destructive only when it tries to take over your tower for itself. A good illustration of this can be found in the much-abused term *self-realization*: when only the ego has a say, it looks

for its own advantage in everything (even in love). Everywhere it looks, it finds only itself, even in the word *self-real-I-zation*.

When you befriend yourself and unite your ego and true self, however, you will find something more hidden in this concept: *self-re-ALL-ization*. Say the word out loud with the two different emphases. You will be surprised how hard *self-real-I-zation* sounds and how friendly and gentle *self-re-ALL-ization* sounds.

Self-Love and Love for Others. Loving your neighbor is worthwhile not only for moral reasons, but also for reasons of self-interest: you will not gain inner riches through yourself alone, but rather through devotion to and sympathy for others. How could you achieve this if you have nothing in your own self to offer others? You shouldn't focus on your "self-realization," but rather on gaining the strength to be there for others. There's a good reason that the Bible says, "Love your neighbor *as* yourself" and not "*instead* of yourself." It is futile to devote yourself to your neighbor unless you love yourself. Your self-love gives you a power that can be given away and spent. We must stop thinking of self-love as egotism.

Enroll in Humor School

Would you have thought that for most people neither money nor good looks are the most important thing they look for in a partner? Kurt Starke, professor at the Leipzig Research Group for Research in Partners and Sexuality, came to the following conclusion after long-term studies with more than 60,000 people: a person's dream partner is intelligent, trustworthy, and empathetic, and—has a sense of humor. According to this sociology professor, finding a funny partner is "the best thing that can happen to someone!"

Stay Healthy—Be Cheerful. Humor represents *strength*, "in a close relationship with vitality, sovereignty, solidarity, friendliness, and also with sensuality and passion. Humorless people are bad lovers." Doctors have further established that laughter can cure the common cold, strengthen the immune system, and increase creativity. So it is also smart from a biological perspective to find a partner with a sense of humor: living with a humorous person at your side is simply healthier than living with a killjoy.

A hearty laugh is an expression of trust and intimacy. The more you trust another person, the more likely you are to laugh with him or her. Cheerfulness goes hand-in-hand with successful flirtation; laughter is a way for you to communicate to each other: "I'm enjoying our time together." The positive feelings you get when you laugh become associated with your flirting partner—and he or she becomes more attractive to you.

Avoid Negative Humor. Here is a simplifying rule of thumb: the healthiest laughter is when you're laughing at yourself. Witty remarks should refer only to yourself. Jokes made at your partner's expense might make other people laugh, but they are actually hurtful to everyone present. It's a short step from humor to sarcasm, and it's easy to hit the wrong tone.

Take a Humor Test with Your Partner. Because behind every joke is a grain of truth, jokes offer you insight into sides of your partner that may not be immediately obvious. Pay attention to what kinds of jokes your partner makes about the opposite sex. What do these jokes say about men and women? Such jokes often give you a better idea of a person's true attitude toward sex, love, and partnership than the "official" opinion he or she expresses. If your partner can enjoy self-deprecating humor and humor that makes fun of his or her own sex, then the prospects are good for your relationship. If, on the other hand, your partner constantly scorns or ridicules your sex, then you had better keep your distance— it's very likely that the jokes will turn on you later in the relationship. Watch out for people who only make jokes at the expense of others!

Become Master of Your Everyday Life

In earlier times, the model marriage looked something like this: the husband can't even boil water, much less use a washing machine and iron, while the wife takes care of the house and understands nothing of money and business: two people completely incapable in certain areas who are forced to band together. Two shaky, crooked towers who must lean on each other to somehow survive.

Learn Beyond Your Own Sex. This outdated model doesn't work anymore. Even at that time the model of the blind and the lame who were supposed to complement each other so fantastically often didn't function at all. A good relationship consists of two towers that can both stand up on their own. It is therefore important to educate yourself in all the important tasks of everyday life: preparing a warm meal, making bank transfers, driving a car and navigating unfamiliar surroundings, buying gifts for family members, dealing with the plumber or painter, making doctor appointments, creating a daily to-do list and

sticking to it, washing the windows, hanging a picture, using the washing machine, ironing, and folding the wash. This list, you can imagine, could go on for quite a while.

Living Alone Is Good Practice. Be wary of a partner who has never really lived alone. When a man moves directly from Hotel Mommy into the comfort zone of his future wife's house, it does not bode well for partnership. Along those lines, the stereotype of the helpless woman in need of protection and longing for the strong shoulder of a man is also not a good basis for a long-term relationship.

This is because a person who relies too much on his or her partner is in a dependant and inferior position. When the one person is never equal with the other, he or she will eventually come to resent the other for this imbalance.

Make Yourself More Attractive

How do you become content and happy with your physical appearance? The following method is safer and quicker than cosmetic surgery, makeup tricks, or laborious fitness programs and will improve your attitude toward your tower's appearance.

Discover Your Beauty. The basic premise for this exercise is inspired by reports of so-called near-death experiences: people who were pronounced clinically dead yet were brought back to life. Most of them report having an out-of-body experience; they stepped out of their body and saw it lying under them, usually from a great height. Almost all of them said that they found their body to be beautiful.

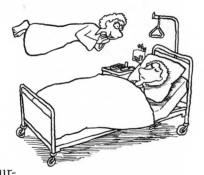

In no way do these people, in the process of dying, see themselves in an exaggeratedly positive light. The famous "life passing before your eyes" is judged surprisingly objectively *and* self-critically. One can easily imagine that the idea of the Last Judgment arose from this self-evaluation of the most important moments of a person's life.

Why do people at the end of their lives judge so self-critically and yet always see their bodies so positively? The explanation is simple: as you glide over into the realm of death, you finally shut out the many outside judgments that have burdened you during your lifetime. When you are completely honest with yourself, you can't help but come to this grand realization: your earthly body is beautiful. It is wholeheartedly you. This body was and is the living space of your spirit. At death, when the ego has nothing more to say, it becomes clear that your spirit loved your body implicitly.

Differentiate Between Beauty and Love. In contrast, in everyday normal life (before the moment of dying) we tend to listen to the ego. Because it likes to make judgments, it very often makes a monumental error: it confuses "beauty" with the right to be loved. From the ideas of your parents to the advertisements in fashion magazines, you are taught the following: only if you are pretty enough will you be loved. Or to look at this the other way around: if no one loves me, it's because I'm not pretty enough. This disastrous association drives young people to extreme eating disorders or to excessive exercising or bodybuilding, into chronic depression or into uncontrolled aggression. Older people compare themselves with their appearance when they were younger and feel isolated and rejected because of their looks.

They have externalized their feelings of self-worth and feel inferior according to their learned value system.

It's a vicious circle of ego-deception: before you feel loved, you must find yourself beautiful; but to feel beautiful, you must be loved. You could continue this spiral until your death, and finally at the point of death, come to see the liberated spirit that you actually had the whole time in your beautiful body. Luckily, there is a way to hold onto this positive truth during your lifetime.

All the defects that you see on your body (e.g., weight problems, acne, thinning hair, wrinkles, etc.) don't originate in your body, but rather in your mind. You can see this in world-famous, flawlessly beautiful models who still think their legs are too fat, their neck is too long, or their eyes are too light. All the problems that you have with your appearance are rooted in your mind, and only there can you solve them.

Shake Up Your Value System. You can't simply shut off your own value system nor silence your inner critic. But as a start, you can destabilize your judgment system. Consider the following thought experiment, where you think of

- Situations in which you were highly praised, although your appearance was anything but attractive
- Unattractive people whom you like and appreciate very much

- Very beautiful people whose stupid or disagreeable behavior made their beauty utterly repulsive
- Famous people whom you admire, but who are not good-looking at all
- Artworks that at first don't correspond to any ideal of beauty but founded a new quality of charm and grace
- Pictures and objects that you find tasteless, but that others consider great works of art
- Something that you found wonderfully beautiful as a child, but today find terribly gaudy

You many come up with some other ideas to further shake up your judgments. In the end, your inner critic should be so irritated that it wants to quit its job. Then you've made the first step.

Experiment with Your Appearance. Even if you've successfully tricked your inner critic for a few minutes, the old, negative thoughts will pop up again after a while (e.g., "I'm so shy, so clumsy, so fat, so pale . . ."). Many people try drugs or alcohol, but the self-confidence that they seem to gain that way is decidedly deceptive, transient, and easily seen through by others. You're better off trusting your body's natural chemical stabilizers: when you get into an unfamiliar, difficult situation, for example, it produces the hormone dopamine. Moderate physical activity strengthens the production of adrenalin. Both substances—in the right dosage—improve your mood and give you a moderate "high." It has been proven that if you intensively think new, unfamiliar thoughts and visualize new, positive situations, your dopamine levels increase. You can try this out in the following activity.

Play the Movie Game. Watch a movie with a hero or heroine who is a positive image for you—ideally in the theater and alone, because this makes for the most intense experience. Abandon yourself, turn off your inner critic, and let yourself identify with George Clooney,

Catherine Zeta-Jones, Cameron Diaz, or whomever. And then leave the theater as George, Catherine, or Cameron. Imagine, as a half-hour experiment, that you have the exact same fantastic charisma as your chosen star. It's best to try this out on total strangers: with the server in a café, with a salesperson, or in small talk at the bus stop. Observe how you walk, how you hold your head high, and how others react to you and maybe turn around to look at you. Not everyone, but some of them. For many people, this experience can be a revolution in itself.

Of course, this effect doesn't last long. But even a small experience can help you find your way out of that "I'm unattractive because I'm unloved because I'm unattractive" trap and transform yourself with a positive trend. After the little games in the café and at the bus stop, try it out in your real life: on the telephone with colleagues or in conversation with friends. You improve yourself and learn to trust your newfound charisma when you practice with people who used to intimidate you.

Once you have started to expose the apparent logic of your "I am unattractive" mechanism, you will never again be as inhibited by it as before. Not everybody will think you're great all of the time, but you will receive positive feedback and acknowledgment that you are always worthy of love. Turns out, the skin that you're in was and will always be beautiful enough.

Simplifying Idea 4:
Prepare Yourself for Love

The best way to become happily formerly single is to dive right into good relationships. Imagine that you can stretch golden ropes of friendship from tower to tower. With just such a rope you will one day bind yourself together with a partner of the heart.

Find Five Friends

Once you've spent some time burrowing into your tower, you will discover that being alone can be painful. Not only your spirit suffers: also your health is endangered because it directly negatively affects your well-being when you spend too little time with other people. Many studies have shown that loneliness increases the risk of heart attack, cancer, and diseases related to weakened immune systems. The University of Ohio has proven that the inverse is also true: people with a good network of stable friendships are also physically better off. The best news of all is you don't need to find hundreds of friends to reap the health benefits!

Just like in Enid Blyton's classic children's series *The Famous Five*, all you need are five close confidants whom you like and see regularly. Relatives don't count! These five friends are the people whom you can rely on when you need help. Just as important, they can always come to you for advice and help. With these five companions you hone important relationship skills that you will always need in a partnership: reliability, respect, humor, trustworthiness, helpfulness, warmth, and self-critique.

Get out of the Loneliness Trap. People who hate being lonely and want to make new friends often come off as being depressed. Through their gloomy attitude, they scare potential friends away; it's a vicious, self-fulfilling cycle. Therefore, our advice may seem like a paradox: if you want to make new friends to not be lonely anymore, you first have to learn to love being alone.

Make friends with yourself. What do you like to do alone? Think of activities that you loved as a child but haven't done for years: building model ships, fishing, singing out loud, tinkering around in the garage, window-shopping, dancing alone to loud music, or whatever your interests are. When you turn this list into action, you do things that bring you joy and improve your mood. Because you are spending positive time with yourself, you learn to better appreciate your own company. By doing so, you become more lovable and interesting to other people.

Our second piece of advice is to act as if you had all the friends in the world. Open your heart to others in anticipation of making new friends. To do so, you have to leave your little room in the tower. Go be among people. Practice first on the bus, at the mall, or at the movies. Imagine that everyone likes you. Smile at people—kids, teenagers, the elderly, salespeople, bus drivers, and lifeguards. Visit public parks and buildings with this friendly feeling, and enjoy even the smallest positive response that you receive. Not everyone will return your smile, but that's not the point. What matters is that you get used to always sending positive signals from your tower. Someday Mr. or Ms. Right will get your signal—and respond!

Keep Your Strengths in Mind. People who sit alone in their tower for too long tend to exaggerate their faults and have poor self-esteem. Having low self-esteem, though, is as unhealthy as not being self-critical enough. Gradually, you will get to know the chambers of your personal tower well. Maybe you have already developed a critical eye toward your weaknesses and have an idea of how to put your best self forward. Maybe you've washed the cobwebs out of your past and made friends with yourself. Now you should get something in return for all your hard work.

> **Simplifying Tip:** Imagine yourself in front of your bathroom mirror with a pad of self-stick notes. Write down all of your positive characteristics on them, and stick these notes all around the mirror: I'm a good listener, I like to laugh, I'm good at recognizing the needs of others, I am good at explaining complicated things, and so on. Each time you look in the mirror, you will see those imaginary self-stick notes, smile, and remember that you're not such a bad person to have around after all. ■

Discover the Friends Whom You Already Have. Remember, there are plenty of people from the past whom you always got along well with. The best of them will still remember you and would be happy to hear from you. True friendship can often be revived even after decades.

> **Simplifying Tip:** When you make contact again, don't go overboard apologizing for not being in touch for so long—your friend didn't reach out to you, either. If you have the feeling that your friend is truly happy to hear from you, go ahead and say straight out: "Let's pick up our old friendship again; it meant so much to me." Or, "I don't want so much time to go by before we talk to each other again." Tell your friend which qualities you especially admire in him or her. By doing so, you show that you don't just think your friend is "nice," but that you're actually interested in a deeper dimension of him or her. ■

Turn off the Sex Button. Many lonely single people immediately seek a possible relationship in every member of the opposite sex they meet. But being overanxious or pushy will make you seem needy and will scare many people away.

> **Simplifying Tip:** Make an effort to make platonic friendships with a few friends of your own sex. This will normalize your interactions with the opposite sex. ■

Make Yourself Useful. People who are lonely often wonder, "Who needs me, anyway?" Or they are one-sidedly fixated on how others could help them. The easiest way out of loneliness, though, is to reach out to others. As a single person, you have more free time, and this flexibility can make you particularly helpful to others. Assisting others strengthens your self-awareness—and will make you feel better too!

> **Simplifying Tip:** Get engaged in community politics, a church, a local charity, or explore clubs in your area. Throw your prejudices out the window. Organizations and associations don't have to be stiff and boring. Plenty of organizations pursue nonprofit, artistic, and aesthetic interests. Statements such as "Getting involved just isn't my thing," are just classic defense mechanisms used by loners who won't get involved for fear of being hurt. ■

Take the Initiative. When you find someone you would like to get to know better, try taking a small step to reach out to that person: "Do you know how late the gym is open?" "Are you waiting for the train?" "Let's grab a bite after the meeting." Don't be pushy, and don't take it too hard if the other person says no. Maybe this just wasn't the best time for that person, and another day would work out better.

> **Simplifying Tip:** Think of the self-stick notes on your bathroom mirror. Imagine that the other person needs to have the right opportunity to get to know all of your good qualities. For this, you need an occasion when the two of you can talk to each other. You can create this opportunity. Even if you try to arrange a meeting that doesn't work out, you've made the first step by taking the initiative. ■

Take Three Steps Toward Yourself

When you're looking for a new path in your search for a partner, try the following strategy, which the psychologist Gay Hendricks suggests. He himself found his true love this way after eight (often tortuous) relationships, and he has now been happily married for more than twenty years. Professor Hendricks discovered that to enter a meaningful partnership, you must first make yourself emotionally available for a long-lasting and fulfilling relationship. There are three prerequisites for this:

Prerequisite 1: Get Rid of Your Guilt. Say good-bye to your conscious or unconscious guilt over your previous, unsuccessful relationships. Unacknowledged guilty feelings get in the way of opening yourself up to a new relationship. Track down your guilt feelings. Say out loud: "Yes, I admit my past mistakes and all their consequences, even if I wasn't able to before. I don't know exactly what has kept me from having a good relationship, but I take full responsibility for my part in that from now on."

Prerequisite 2: Make a Confession. Stop pretending that you find single life "great" or "just fine." Around 90 percent of single people want a long-term, preferably lifelong partnership. If you truly belong to the 7 percent of absolutely happy single people, then pass this book on to someone else! If not, admit to yourself: "Yes, I want a relationship with all my heart. I really want this." Be sure to let all of your cool single friends know, too.

Prerequisite 3: Make a Commitment to Yourself. Can you keep a promise? Honor a contract that you've signed? Just as these can be difficult to follow through on, it's just as difficult to form a deep and fulfilling relationship and share your everyday life with another person. If you can't put pressure on yourself, can't stand confrontation, and don't have a healthy dose of self-discipline, then you're going to have a tough time finding lasting happiness. Say out loud: "Yes, I want a loving relationship, even if I have to make sacrifices for it. It's worth it to me."

Set Your Sights on Love

When you have made it through these three preparatory steps, you can begin Gay Hendricks's program to reset your heart and mind and open up to love. Hendricks has helped thousands of single people with his three resetting steps and is convinced that the technique works. His suggestions are as simple as they are radical:

Reset 1: A Promise. Promise yourself wholeheartedly that you will bring a new kind of relationship into your life. For this you must ask yourself the following two questions, and answer both with a definite yes as if you were doing it in public—like a bride and groom before the justice of the peace or pastor.

- Do you want a truly loving relationship?
- Do you solidly desire and intend to enter wholeheartedly into a completely new relationship that gives you complete contentment?

Only when you can make these unconditional promises will you be able to achieve what you desire.

If you can't answer these two questions with an unqualified yes, then you are harboring some opposition to a relationship deep inside you. Try saying the following sentence a few times, "At the moment, I, [your name], want to be single/divorced/in a less happy relationship. This is what I am choosing." If this sentence resonates more with you, then your life right now does in fact correspond to what you really prefer (if unconsciously) at the moment.

Be honest with yourself! There is no sense in lying to yourself or pretending.

Reset 2: Absolute Yeses and Nos. This resetting is about bringing to light your true relationship desires that are buried deep inside of you. It's not about looks, age, income, social status, and so on. It's about inner qualities whose presence in a loved one can bring joy and enthusiasm to your spirit every day. They are the basis for a rich inner life as a couple and for the nourishing feeling of a loving, supportive bond.

Which three qualities are absolute must-haves for you in a partner?

> **Simplifying Tip:** Make a long list of inner qualities that your partner absolutely must have. But remember that you can't expect someone else to fulfill something that you haven't already given to yourself. These qualities, then, have to be shared qualities that you live by as well, such as honesty, creativity, humor, reliability, consistency, helpfulness, and modesty. Choose the three that are most important to you.
>
> What are three qualities you absolutely could not live with? ■

This is the other question you need to ask yourself: Which negative qualities can you absolutely not live with in a partner? The equality principle applies here, too: you, too, must be free of these negative qualities yourself. Again, make a longer list of qualities such as aggression, jealousy, messiness, idleness, addiction, dishonesty, or unethical dealings with money, and choose three absolute nos from it.

Now you know your priorities for your partner—the absolute yes and no qualities you are looking for. With these forming the base, you can wish for a few "extras": What other qualities would be nice to have in your love? Think of your preferences. What excites you in the opposite sex? What would be a great gift in another person? Write these qualities on your "wish list" as desirable but not absolutely necessary characteristics. Now you have in black and white what you are really looking for in the kingdom of love.

Reset 3: Let It Flow. The secret of the third resetting is that you can only experience true love when you have filled yourself with love. To do so, you must accept and love yourself unconditionally, and love even those parts of you that are the most difficult for you to love.

Name your fears, your self-criticisms, and your feelings of inferiority. Where do you need love the most? Take a deep breath. Imagine that love is flowing into you. Allow love to flow to that point where you can't love yourself. Don't struggle against this flow or fight it with your thoughts (e.g., "It won't work anyway," "I'm not worthy of love"), but rather love yourself for the fact that you don't know how to love yourself yet.

> **Simplifying Tip:** If you can't let your own love flow right away, imagine instead the eternal cosmic love of the whole universe flowing into you and surrounding you with loving acceptance. ▪

The Second Dwelling of Love
The Love Tent

Your Simplifying Dream: The Love Tent

It is now evening. You stand on the balustrade of your tower and gaze into the darkening sky. The first stars are visible. You notice a strange ache inside you that grows stronger. A primal strength, which you have always felt and that pulls you toward the infinite reaches of the universe, takes on a special energy under the night sky.

Then you see a light in the distance. It shimmers softly and beckons, attracting you with all its power, just like the mysterious shimmering of the tower windows. But now you feel a burning within you. You simply can't remain up in your tower. You storm down the stairs, tear open the door, and rush out into the open toward that light.

The distance is farther than it seemed, but at last you reach the light. It beams from out of the half-open entrance of a beautiful tent. The tent is a light structure of fine cloth, supported by gold-tipped poles, and an exquisite banner flutters at the top. It's a noble tent, fit for the kings and queens of old. Everything about it is delicate and strangely ancient, yet the tent seems as if it were erected just at this moment. Carefully, you peek though the flap to get a glimpse of the interior. It looks like something out of a fairy tale: soft pillows and silk blankets rest on luxurious carpets and delectable food and drinks are ready. An alluring scent envelops you, as if the tent itself gave off an air of contentment. All of your senses are awake, but at the same time confused and beguiled by so much beauty. Suddenly you are certain that someone is waiting for you inside. Your heart thumps; you hesitate, doubt, and feel weak; yet you are more full of energy than ever before. A sweet power pulls you inside, and you are finally ready to let yourself be carried by it.

What kind of force is this that has such power over us? Behind every attractive force in the universe lies a physical power that pervades all aspects of life. For a planet, we call this gravity. This force makes life on Earth possible. It controls our oceans, makes sure the atmosphere doesn't dissipate out into space, and keeps our planet in orbit around the sun, our single source of energy. At the same  time, this power ensures that each electron orbits its atomic nucleus and that molecules combine to form matter. Attraction is the basic principle of our entire world. At the beginning of the universe, there was probably nothing other than this power—and an inconceivable amount of energy.

This power of attraction, which rules our souls, is called love. We find certain ideas, things, or people attractive. Everything originates from this power: our selves, children, language, culture, cities, wars, happiness, and misery. In the center of the universe and in the center of our lives, we find nothing other than this one enticing power: love.

In an international study, psychologist David Buss, together with more than fifty of his colleagues, asked 10,000 people from thirty-seven different cultures which qualities were the most important to them in a life partner. Across all nations and for both men and women, one quality was consistently at the top of the list: mutual attraction and love.

This is the power that beckons you from your tower. Although you've made your tower so comfortable, your soul rebels against the confines of your lonely self and searches for opportunities to develop and grow. It achieves this with the most effective means possible: through the power of attraction. Nothing in the world can now hold you back from falling in love.

Simplifying Idea 5: Follow Your Desire

The exotic, intimate, airy love tent represents the thrilling, unbelievable lightness of being in love. No other dwelling of love gives you so much mobility and such a feeling of freedom as this tent. When you're in love, you have hope. It activates your internal and external energies to the maximum extent. Love functions within you as a spiritual power superior to your conscious ego. You can do brave things and perform bold acts that you wouldn't normally be able to do. Love might inspire you to start a completely new life, to eventually "break down your tent" and move in with someone. At no other point in your life do you feel so free, so lighthearted, so boundless as when you are happily in love.

The Campsite: Your Place Among the Heavens

At the same time, however, a new love can be tender and fragile. This is part of the reason we've chosen a tent as the symbol of this phase. In contrast to the solid foundation of the tower, a tent's thin cloth walls of emotions and desires make it extremely delicate and sensitive. Lovers blindly follow their own hearts. As a lover, you

have the luxury of seeing only yourself and your partner, nothing else. At the same time, you can see more than other people can. You see everything: the universe, the oneness of all things. You are one with the stars, floating timeless in space, and you can linger in the most exquisite moments.

Lovers with their tents are "traveling folk." Camping out in the tent fills you with wonder. You are closer to nature, freedom, and adventure. The love tent entices you with an irresistible promise of things visible and invisible, strange and familiar. Infatuated lovers hang their boundless expectations on this promise. Because of it, they can for a moment forget all the protective and defensive mechanisms they brought with them from their towers. They don't let themselves be hemmed in by social norms and expectations. They forget the cultural rules that otherwise keep them grounded and secure. People in love are therefore also much more fragile and less stable. They often feel powerless and defenseless before the person they love. A small storm of feeling can be enough to make a newly constructed love tent collapse. One must learn to tread carefully around such a fragile emotional structure.

The Tent Walls: Your Dreams

Why does your spirit call up so much passion and creative energy? You produce an inner image of love with all your power, and then you project it on the walls of another person's tent. This *imago amore* is charged with positive energy from your subconscious. Then a miracle happens: a completely unknown person suddenly becomes interesting and desirable. Your beloved is surrounded with mystery. He or she is everything that you are not and that you desire. Your beloved is the stuff of your dreams. This person miraculously corresponds to the image of your desire—and this is all the more true the less you know the person! This projection game works the best when the other person emanates a "promising uncertainty" (C. G. Jung). This leaves you free to project all the positive qualities you wish you had onto that person. When you're near your beloved, you feel nobler and stronger, freer and more alive. This gives the infatuation phase its intensity. Later, when you move out of the love tent, you experience the opposite: you abolish your projections and allow real love into your consciousness. When you do this, you mature, establish a more definite relationship, and differentiate your individual self more clearly.

At the beginning, of course, you don't give a thought to any of this. You are fascinated and intoxicated, a little crazy and out of control. You long for nothing more than to be together at every moment so this exquisite state may never end.

Inside the Tent: Your Temple

When you're infatuated, you experience a series of spiritual miracles. Latent parts of your personality spontaneously awaken, and you are overwhelmed with feelings. The nearness of the other person confuses and quickens you at the same time. The gates of your unconscious are wide open; you are extremely receptive not only for anything emotional and sensual, but also for spiritual experiences. Many mystics use the language of love when they speak of God, and lovers speak in mystical images. Love has a mystical dimension, and you come very close to this in the love tent. Here, your soul sings its singular love song. In the infatuation phase, you trust your soul like never before. It rewards you immediately, allowing tremendous energies to flow into you. You float in oceanic images and emotions; you feel as if you could put your arms around the whole world—your love is boundless, of cosmic proportions. Everything is magical, everything is possible, everything is holy.

Love is holy, and God, the holiest of holies, is love. This is why the house of God in the human soul resembles the love tent. The Latin name for tent may be known to those of you familiar with the Catholic Church: *tabernaculum*—tabernacle. Every lover and every pair of lovers is a living tabernacle or temple for love, for the "sacrament of the moment" (Jean-Pierre de Caussade), the limitless devotion to another in the here and now.

The Three-Starred Banner: Eros, Amor, and Agape

We place our greatest hopes in love. The classical symbol for hope is the star. People dream of reading the future in the stars. They hope that a good star stands over their relationship. The star is a kind of fingerprint of hope upon our spirit. Therefore, it must also be present in the love tent.

Perhaps you already noticed that a flag was hoisted over your tower. It symbolizes that your spirit is at home in the tower (just like the Union Jack is raised above Buckingham Palace when the Queen is in London).

Two such banners fly over the love tent. Each of you has brought a flag and raised it above the tent as a sign that not only are you physically present, but you've also brought your spirit with you. Each flag has three stars, symbolizing a unique separation of the different kinds of love.

What we refer to with the word *love* had two different names in ancient times: *eros* and *agape* (by the Greeks) or (by the Romans) *amor* and *caritas*. Today, we have *romantic love* and *altruism*. In the work of mythologist Joseph Campbell, we found a three-part division that was very illuminating for us: *eros*, *amor*, and *agape*. In mythology, Amor is actually just the Latin translation of the god of love, but as you will see in a moment, a few significant differences can be very helpful for you in your own love tent.

Eros, the Star of Attraction. Eros is the pop star of our time. He provides the primal cosmic power of seduction and mutual attraction. This is very concrete, since Eros is the chemist and the optician, responsible for everything that stimulates you erotically: figure, voice, movement, clothing, dance, scent, touch, image, music, film, and text. Eros is the urge that overwhelms your body. He guides your drives and hormones; he is responsible for sexual desire and physical union. Not surprisingly, he is often considered quite dangerous. For centuries, he was held in check by only being allowed to appear within the strict confines of countless taboos. The erotic areas of men's and women's bodies are covered in everyday life. In many cultures today, women still are completely covered and allowed access to only certain areas of life.

Eros himself is driven by instinct and thus is not very picky. He changes partners easily and thinks rather superficially. For him, anyone can get together with anyone, as long as their signals match. Eros wants sex and satisfaction, affairs and adventures—no solid commitments. He also doesn't really suffer when one lover departs—he rebounds quickly from such losses. Eros alone is not enough for a lasting love, although his wild-animal power and devoted passion are absolutely essential for it.

Amor, the Star of Unique Love. Something completely different happens when your spirit also is attracted to the unique personality of another person. In our three-part division of love, Amor is the guy with the arrow. In contrast to Eros, he is extremely picky. His guiding principle is exclusivity. The heart must speak—for both people! This is the revolutionary idea of romantic love, which has entrenched itself deeply over the past few hundred years into our Western consciousness.

When you are hit by Amor's arrow, you experience the "spiritual impact of love," as Joseph Campbell calls it. It doesn't get any more unique than this. Love wounds your heart, and only this one person can heal you. This person is not exchangeable. He or she is your destiny. You want to explore and know this person's innermost being. You have the feeling you've known this person since the dawn of time. You want to look into this person's heart, comprehend his or her true being, and open your soul to this person.

Amor's arrow strikes and wounds. He leaves your heart "lovesick." It seems as if your future life with this person is already whispering to you: "This is the one! It's this person and no one else." Amor is the most personal star of love. His goal is for a couple to penetrate deeper and deeper into the core of each other's beings. It can ripen into the highest spiritual experience of eternal unity. All great lovers in our Western culture are Amor's creatures: Orpheus and Eurydice, Pyramus and Thisbe, Abelard and Heloise, Romeo and Juliet, Dante and Beatrice, Faust and Gretchen.

Agape, the Star of Selfless Love. The third star on the banner is Agape, the Greek name for a selflessly giving love. Here we once again have a more general and socially oriented form of love. Agape shows herself in your readiness to devote yourself to other people, to "love your neighbor as yourself." She goes beyond herself, even beyond the couple, and cares selflessly for others, even for complete strangers, since your neighbor can indeed be anyone. With Agape, you live the opposite of egoism, putting yourself on the back burner. Thanks to Agape, you don't have your own well-being in mind, but rather that of others. You see what potential lies in your partner, and you help him or her to unlock it. You not only support your partner, but also cultivate good family relationships and friendships, take care of your children and your parents, do charity work, or fill in for a sick colleague.

Agape means making another person your highest priority out of your own free will, while also treating that person with the utmost respect. The old Church Fathers saw this as a symbol of the boundless love of God to humans, and thus the word agape also refers to the "love feast" of the early Christian churches. In an expression of mutual love, people come together in a communal feast, to which each person brings something to share. With Agape, you cultivate a sense of community and the selfless aspects of your partnership. Agape opens your heart for empathy and brings benevolence into your relationship. Whenever you take responsibility for others in a generous, committed way, Agape lights up on your banner.

What the Starred Banner Is Good For. Three kinds of love instead of one—at first glance, this doesn't exactly seem like simplification. But this division of that wonderful thing called love can really simplify your love life:

- *Assess the future of your relationship.* Many relationships fail despite the fact that Amor and Eros are in splendid harmony for both parties: because one partner feels that the other does nothing for their love. He or she is infatuated and very interested in physical and emotional closeness. But when love between two people is left hanging and doesn't move past mere physical intimacy, it soon loses its power and suffocates both of them. The guiding power of Agape is missing. In each lover, an unconscious "testing" program is always running: "Can my partner protect or care for me in an emergency?" "Can I raise children with him?" "Will she tackle the homestead with me?" In short, "Does he or she support me in everyday life?" This may seem unromantic, but when this third kind of love is present in a relationship, Eros and Amor receive one more powerful shove. Agape is the down-to-earth ingredient missing in many "Hollywood marriages."

■ *Understand how your love develops.* Think of the three stars of love as an hourglass. On top is Eros, the more general romantic energy, a kind of magnetism that at some point awakens in each man and woman and may depend on trivial things: he's crazy for long hair, high heels, or freckles. She's into strong muscles, slender hands, or a particular cologne. On this level, all sorts of people can be an option. But in the middle of the hourglass, the energy of love narrows. Here only one person can make it through. Here the lightning of affection strikes and the power of attraction explodes. Further down, the hourglass widens out again, encompassing others and longing to be shared. These three movements trade off, mix together, and strengthen one another. When the erotic attraction in a partnership dies down, the star of Amor or Agape usually shines brighter. But if you're still looking through the lens of Eros, you won't be able to see this.

Test Your Love Lights

In your relationship, all three stars of love should find their place and work together. If only two of them are shining or just one, then it's time to find the reason for those missing or fading stars. Doing this is simplest with our Love Light test. It's best to answer the following questions, separately at first and in writing. Afterward, you can discuss your results with each other.

Before you start this conversation, read and sign the following statement in your mind: I will be open. I will not injure you or accuse you. Please listen, even if you are shocked at first. Only in this way can we make the wonderful stars of our love shine again.

The Eros Love Light Test: How attractive does my partner make himself for me? What do I do to make sure he finds me attractive and erotically exciting? What do I find seductive, enticing, and beguiling about him? What does he find enchanting about me? What makes it spark between us? How do we recognize that we desire each other? Which external conditions support this? Which one of us is active in seduction, and which of us is passive? Is my passionate desire directed at my partner?

The Amor Love Light Test: What constitutes the uniqueness of my feelings for her? What distinguishes this person from all other potential partners whom I have encountered? Does what she says really refer to me personally or could she just as easily be talking to someone else? Is she interested in my individual personality? Am I "the one" for her? Do I want to discover and get to know her innermost self? Does she try to see into my heart? Does she understand me so well that the things she says about me go straight to my heart? Do I myself know my partner this well?

The Agape Love Light Test: How thoughtful, compassionate, and supportive is my partner with other people? How supportive and thoughtful were his family? How is he with his friends? Does he offer help? How does he respond to the suffering and need of others? Who has the benefit of his compassion and care? What does he do without being asked (in practical and concrete terms) when I'm having a hard time?

Ask yourself these questions the other way around: How much of this do I practice myself? Do I recognize the needs of my partner? How selfless can I be? Where would I draw the line? Answer these questions honestly and with the awareness that you can't expect anything from your partner that you don't practice yourself.

Simplifying Tip: To start your conversation together, imagine that the night sky is arching over your love tent. Tell yourself which love stars you saw twinkling during the three parts of your Love Light test. Set these stars in your banner, and admire their light together. ■

Make Your Stars Shine. Each love thrives on sweet, trivial things and surprising moments. Make "star days" out of your everyday life: when one of you sees one of the three relationship stars lighting up, he or she gets to declare the day a star day. Here are a few ideas we found in novels, films, advice books, and on the Internet:

■ *What you can do for Eros's light:* Go swimming and have your partner float in the water while you comb her hair (be careful!) or help him shave (be very careful!); give tender massages with fine oils; buy luxuriant bedding and lingerie together; invent an erotic love code of gestures and words; photograph, paint, or sculpt each other; and talk about your sexual desires.

■ *What you can do for Amor's light:* Write love letters instead of just calling on the phone; trade off watching favorite films; find new favorite places together (e.g., a park bench, a tree, a restaurant, a lake, a field); learn something new together; look at childhood photos of each other and tell stories about them; tell each other what you dreamed the night before; give a love poem; fulfill a childhood wish of your partner; and talk about moving in together and marrying.

■ *What you can do for Agape's light:* go shopping for your partner; cook, clean up, or wash the dishes; wash the other's car, vacuum it, and fill up the gas tank; accompany the other to an unpleasant appointment or commitment; teach the other how to do something that you can do well; help friends together; study for a test with your partner; take care of your partner when he or she is sick; take an interest in your partner's family and visit them; and talk about your desire for children.

How Many Tents Should You Build?

As delightful as those ecstatic experiences in the love tent may be, all too often two people have to admit that they can't stay together for the long term. They break down their tent with sorrow and tears and hope for their next chance. This raises some questions: How often should you move into a new love tent? How many partners should you have had before marriage or a lifelong relationship? In the past, the answer was hard but simple: sexual union was synonymous with life-long union (although if you looked closer, you would see that in practice this often was not strictly the case).

How Useful Is Sexual Experience? Today, things are different. Sexual liberation has certainly brought us some advantages. Women as well as men are allowed to have fun with sex and are no longer persecuted by the guardians of public morals. Yet this sexual freedom also has negative effects on the spirit (e.g., adultery, frequent change of partners, AIDS, abortion)—something that has been played down for a long time. Psychologist C. G. Jung prophesied as early as 1930 that "the unavoidable outcome will be that personal relationships between the sexes will suffer. Easy access [to sexuality] doesn't challenge our character values and thus also does not develop them, and at the same time it presents an obstacle for deep mutual understanding, which must be taken seriously."

In the language of the three stars of love, this means the more you position Eros as your sole broker of love, the less Amor will be called upon to help bring a man and woman together. The more easily men and women are accepted as sexual partners, the less Agape-effort they must exert to qualify as romantic partners for the opposite sex. It is easy to find a replacement when one person withdraws or refuses sexual favors. Building up a personal relationship becomes more and more superfluous, because the satisfaction of one's own needs gains primacy. Love deflates and ends, according to Jung, in "fleeting sexual interludes": Eros suppresses Amor and Agape.

Jung also described further consequences for men: their personal development slackens. The understanding depth of feeling that gives a man's soul an inner weight and that women so long for isn't sufficiently cultivated under the sole reign of Eros. So it happens that many young men, thanks to Eros, live the sexuality of an adult while retaining the spirit of a child. Their spiritual and emotional puberty, according to Jung's experience, is still not finished by age twenty-five or even older. Only with Amor's help does a man become spiritually and emotionally adult—because Amor wounds his heart by opening it for one particular woman. Only with Agape's help can a man fully and completely do his part in a relationship.

Don't Place Too Much Importance on Sexual Experience. Today we can see that C. G. Jung's observations also apply to women. They, too, stumble quickly without enough thought put into their sexual relationships. Sexual experience and emotional competence, though, are something different. This doesn't mean that you're not allowed to have any sexual experiences at all before entering a long-term partnership or marriage, as conservative circles in particular may demand. Siegfried Schnabl, the most famous sex researcher in the former East Germany, sees in these old purity rules a misanthropic attitude toward sex that was primarily directed at women: "as if having sex made a girl unclean." Part of developing a healthy sense of self involves becoming acquainted with and developing your own sexuality free from fear and pressure.

Simplify Your Sexuality: Be Monogamous. It's no accident that monogamous relationships have come to prevail in human history. Having multiple liaisons at once or frequently changing partners costs an enormous amount of energy, nerves, and time. In the age of AIDS, these things are also potentially very dangerous. Concentrating on one partner is the best way to realize your own potential to love with respect to body, spirit, and soul. Gay Hendricks, professor of psychotherapy and relationship specialist (mentioned in Chapter 1), advocates marriage wholeheartedly: "Monogamy is the only thing, in my experience, that works." Hendricks is convinced that commitment to a serious relationship is the beginning of a spiritual path. This decision releases an inner strength that sets a mysterious dynamic into motion, as mutual unrestricted commitment between partners fosters trust. This gives both partners the freedom to bring their unsettled shadow sides into the light of consciousness. When a commitment is viewed by both partners as binding, both make the effort to clear up problems in the relationship. They grapple with each other and mature together.

Sex Opens up a Door. When you become sexually involved with each other, you throw open the door to deep, intense experiences. Sex is a powerful key to your inner world. Sex is about closeness, fundamental trust, and readiness to commit. It touches upon our most basic relationship desires and concerns, especially the painful experience of being apart. Imagine your inner desires in the following way: you wait longingly in front of a door that opens itself. A sexual union opens what was closed before. For a moment, all separation is suspended. Sex signals to your heart and your soul that you have the ability to form a deep relationship. That's why sex is so attractive, not because it releases some hormones!

Simplifying Idea 6: Actively Seek a Life Partner

Even if it sometimes doesn't seem that way, we actually live in one of the most romantic epochs in history. Seldom before has the belief in the power of love been greater or the trust in the pinpoint accuracy of Amor's arrow stronger. One day we will meet the person who is meant for us—this dream slumbers in many hearts. This even goes for people who have just experienced a breakup. Yes, sometimes it is even this very dream that leads to the breakup: the idea that out there somewhere a person is waiting who suits us even better. Polls of young people sug-

gest, however, that our society gradually is moving past the golden age of this romantic ideal. People are once again going about things more purposefully.

This is our advice for simplification: deromanticize romance so that love can have a chance. Don't think of a clever strategy and a bit of planning as something unnatural. You won't botch up Amor's handi-work—rather, you'll work intelligently with him.

Where to Meet People

This territory has been explored quite thoroughly. Taking a look at current trends shows that, most often, the sparks fly at

work. In second place is your circle of friends. The Internet has been undisputed in third place since 2003. Virtual dating services have surpassed even the classic meeting places such as bars and dance clubs. We have sorted our simplification tips according to the order of this hit parade of love.

Searching for a Partner at the Workplace. Most couples meet along the career path. Still, not every office flirtation ends happily—a few people even have in the end lost not only their desired partner but also their job. It's important to know the rules of the game so that you don't run into any on-the-job hazards.

- *Widen your radius.* Enlarge the circle of people with whom you interact. If you work in a small company, use every opportunity to work outside the office. Visit in person business partners whom you usually only talk to on the phone. Your company could profit from this, and the most important person of your life just might cross your path!

  If you work in a large firm, don't stay holed up in your division. Use the existing infrastructure: go to continuing education classes, take on small office responsibilities (e.g., distributing supplies, helping organize the company picnic, etc.).

■ *Don't fall into the hierarchy trap.* Flirt with a colleague rather than with your boss. Sticking to your own level ensures equality in the relationship, and in general that is good for love: you can be sure that the other person isn't just returning your signals because he or she hopes to get some career boost out of it. Also, in the case of a breakup, your job isn't in danger.

■ *Accept rejection.* Really. If you ignore a clear refusal, you could be accused of sexual harassment in the workplace— legal action could follow.

■ *Don't make a show of your relationship.* Don't annoy your colleagues. Constantly dropping by, calling on the phone, or holding hands gets on other people's nerves as much as does that person who's always five minutes late to the meeting or the other who always yawns loudly all morning. Every task that goes unfinished because of your romance costs you empathy points.

■ *Break up with dignity.* The greatest dangers for your job aren't lurking during your office liaison, but after it! If the relationship falls apart, it's important that you both find your way back into your original colleague roles. Maintain mutual respect, and remain discreet. Don't vent your anger about your ex in front of your other colleagues, as tempting as it may be. Reduce your daily contact with your ex as much as you can. If you have to, have yourself transferred. The best distraction is to throw yourself into your work so your performance doesn't suffer.

Searching for a Partner in Your Social Circle. Not every workplace is a very social environment, and many people long for a person with whom they share more of their private life. Besides, you also avoid the pitfalls of an on-the-job romance when you look to your social surroundings. After a breakup, many friendships fall apart, and your need for outside contacts drops off at first. In that case, the following principle for simplification goes especially for you: don't sit around and suffer—do something; be active, not passive.

- *Bar acquaintances—no, thank you.* Dance clubs and trendy bars, the classic meeting places for people looking for a new partner,

  are the least suited to finding serious potential partners (and in the long term, it can get downright expensive). With the loud music, you can hardly have a conversation, and your possibilities have been preselected: you'll find few nonsmokers in a bar, as well as few early risers or health nuts.

- *Vacation romance—better not.* It may sound cruel for us to discourage this. But the chances of meeting your life's partner on the beach or at the breakfast buffet at the hotel are slim.

  In these places, you meet people in that special vacation mood. Far away from home, the temptation to not be yourself is great. At a spa or under the tropical sun, good husbands suddenly become love-hungry singles, and respectable wives discover their lust for adventure. On the other hand, there are no laws in love, only probabilities.

- *Everyday encounters—yes, please.* It will serve you better to attend events you are interested in. Look around in community colleges, sports clubs, or church groups, where the desperate search for a partner isn't your main focus, and the chances for making real contacts isn't so bad. Choose courses or programs that don't take years to complete, so you can get to know a variety of people. Larger events where the participants belong to similar occupational or private areas are also very good, such as trade shows, openings, and conferences.

- *Think against the grain.* Attend gatherings where your gender is underrepresented: men in self-discovery groups, women in sports clubs, and so on. Rediscover the other gender in yourself; put yourself on the "other side." If you are a man who can read a women's magazine, or a woman who can read a car magazine, without thinking everything in it is dumb, you have a giant advantage over your fellow partner-seekers!

- *Use the official trick.* An official function or position helps overcome shyness. Help out for a while serving refreshments at a large festival or greeting new arrivals with a name tag on your shirt. This makes it easier to meet people. Make sure that you're not trapped in your job the entire time, though. Once your shift is over, you have the ideal starting point for a conversation (e.g., "You had such a nice laugh when I was pouring you that beer just now . . ."). Especially effective here is a uniform (that was always Grandpa's trick!).

- *Find a wardrobe adviser.* What should you wear? What looks the best on you? Women often misjudge what men find attractive about them, and vice versa. Find people to advise you, but not only from your own gender. You will be amazed what the other side recommends! Use this seemingly paradoxical idea from behavioral therapy: nothing helps combat shyness so much as an eye-catching outfit.

- *Pay attention to your appearance.* Another useful insight from behavioral psychology: stand up straight, make yourself tall (for women, high heels can help), hold your head turned slightly up, and always breathe consciously and deeply. This way, your body sends a positive signal to your brain: "I am somebody." That has an immediate effect on your surroundings.

Simplifying Tip: If you are shy or nervous, you come off as much more serious than you think. But if you have to force yourself to seem cheerful, things can also go awry. So give others a friendly smile, as if you've already known and liked them a long time. Imagine that you've already had a pleasant and intimate conversation with the person you want to talk to. This way, you achieve exactly the right friendly, relaxed facial expression that makes conversation easier for both of you. ■

Finding a Partner over the Internet. In the 31–40 age group, one out of every two people looking for a partner is looking online. A research project at the University of Zurich explored "the emergence of romantic relationships online" in 2003. More than four thousand members of the Swiss website Partnerwinner were interviewed. The result?

In your immediate surroundings you encounter around 500 potential partners.

Twenty-three percent had found a serious romantic relationship through this site. There were no differences between relationships that were formed over the Internet and those that came about in more conventional ways. Even if we have to take such claims with a grain of salt (a friendly reply to a survey just to stop receiving any more advertisements, or relationships that weren't actually long-term), even if the numbers were only half as high, they would still be sensational. Online dating isn't just popular; it's also effective. Here are the most reliable simplifying tips to improve your chances of success.

- *Take advantage of the vast selection.* Millions of adults aged 18–69 aren't in a serious relationship. Studies show that many of them are not single by choice. That means millions of people are searching for a stable, long-term commitment!
- *Pay attention to serious offers.* The dating services on the Internet can be divided into two main groups, which you

should not confuse: the first category is the more noncommittal online dating, often found under the keywords "sexual encounters." There are singles forums (a kind of electronic bulletin board that anyone can read) and singles

On the Internet the largest matchmaking service can find you more than 500,000.

chats (online flirting via the keyboard). Here you should only take part under a false name and identity. It's more personal with text-message flirts (the exchange of text messages over your cell phone) and voice flirts (directly talking on the phone). In addition to these are a large number of services that expressly advertise "erotic adventures." Our advice for simplification: seeking out erotic adventures (online or direct), one-night stands, or extramarital affairs is guaranteed to make your life complicated. It's extremely rare that an erotic adventure becomes the love of your life.

For this reason, we strongly recommend the second category: online dating services "for long-term relationships." The term *matchmaking* has come to stand for this category. A bit less specific is the expression "online personal ads," which can be used for both categories. Among the matchmakers, several serious services have established themselves. They create detailed personality profiles and search in their giant databases for people with a high number of shared qualities.

There are also singles services for specific groups: single parents, the chronically ill, people older than fifty, churchgoers, and so on. Tips for Internet services quickly become out of date. You'll always find the best current overview on the Internet itself.

- *Be honest.* Even though the temptation is great when you're online, don't represent yourself as someone you're not. Answer the questionnaires to the best of your knowledge and in good faith. Don't make false claims. If you're not a wine expert or don't have a washboard stomach, then you don't want a partner who's looking for just that—you want someone who would be happy to drink a beer with you, love to go for a walk together, or shares your religious views.

- *Expand your circle.* A tip from Arndt Roller, head of Parship, an online dating service in Germany: many single people think too locally or too regionally in their search for a partner. They limit themselves too narrowly and look for their dream partner only within a radius of thirty to sixty miles (50 to 100 km). When they do this, suitable partners with even better "matching points" slip through the net. A greater geographic radius is the simplest way to dramatically improve your chances.

- *Keep an open mind.* A matchmaking service's questionnaire will ask you about the characteristics you're looking for in a partner. Consider friendships that you've had: What do you especially appreciate? What bothers you? Concentrate on the three absolute yeses and nos (see the section Set Your Sights on Love in Chapter 1). You should remain open to everything else—be inclusive!

- *Start with small talk.* Here is a simplifying idea for online dating services: you write back and forth for so long that you've almost already fallen in love. With this, you spare yourself the first "blind" dates that cost you time and wear out your nerves. Internet partner searches rely upon e-mail. If you really can't stand this mode of communication, then you should probably choose another kind of partner search.

  Don't discount small talk about the little annoyances of everyday life as too superficial for the first e-mail. It offers you the opportunity to approach the other person, whom you know very little about at first, in a casual way—at a pace that you determine. Start out by operating only in the realm of topics in which you feel emotionally confident. Don't charge out of the gate like a bull with your conversation partner, and don't start out with a big life confession. This way, you'll protect yourself from avoidable injuries.

Parship's Arndt Roller advises that the most common mistake men make is that they communicate too little, write too short or cool e-mails, and push too quickly for a telephone call or a meeting. So our rule of thumb for simplification is to make an effort when you're writing, think over your answer for a few hours, and read everything over with some distance before you finally send it.

The most common mistake the Parship people observe in women is that their expectations are too high. They expect fantastic qualities from their future partner and break off contact at the first little faux pas. The simplifying rule of thumb for women: don't assume too much deeper meaning, remain sympathetic, and ask before you let yourself get irritated.

- *Give yourself time.* There is a tendency (especially for experienced online daters) to jump into direct contact over the phone. Our advice for simplification is, don't rush it. Even if you find yourself wanting to talk on the phone or meet right after that first short e-mail, hold off. One of the main advantages of Internet dating is that somewhat uncomfortable phase of writing—because it acts as the first filter. This way, you can sort out the unserious and disingenuous offers right off the bat.

- *Protect yourself.* Longing and tender words can fog the brain, but you should always protect your anonymity. Women especially should not give out their name, place of employment, exact location, or anything else that could  definitively identify them. Anyone who presses for such personal information is suspicious! When it comes to phone calls, the man should e-mail his telephone number and have the woman call him. We recommend that the woman block her telephone number from showing up on his caller ID.

- *Safety rules for the first date.* You'll find imposters, con men, and good-for-nothings on the Internet just like you do in regular life. They won't have a chance, though, if you are more alert and clever than they are. Don't rely on e-mail agreements, but instead make plans over the telephone. It's easier to tell how trustworthy someone is by his or her voice than with a text message or e-mail.

  It's especially important for women that you meet in a populated public area of your choosing, a place that you know. In a bad situation, it's good to know the way to the bathrooms and the back exit. Don't feel guilty about sneaking away from a pushy or creepy partner. It's also best to have your first date during the day or early evening in a café—so you can quickly go your separate ways if necessary.

  Tell your relatives or friends where and with whom you are meeting. Don't let yourself be talked into a last-minute change of location on the first date. If you do change your plans, send a text message with the new location. A favorite safety trick of women is to have a girlfriend call during the date and to have a code prepared. For example, "Don't forget—we're supposed to go swimming tomorrow!" really means "This guy is terrible, please come immediately 'by chance' to the café and join us!"

  In a rush of emotion, many people let themselves get carried away into actions that they wouldn't ever have thought possible. Don't laugh at the following pieces of advice; they apply to both men and women equally: Never let yourself get talked into lending money. On no account should the first date take place at your home. Don't ride in the other person's car. Don't accept gifts.

- *Don't expect too much from the first date.* Dress appropriately for the occasion in a casually fashionable and, above all, neat manner. Be prepared for the first look to be a little disappointing. Your fantasy has already filled in the missing information about the person to form your own inner picture of him or her—now it must give way to

reality. If you realize, though, that you really don't fit together, it is acceptable to end the date after a considerate period of fifteen to thirty minutes.

If you are still uncertain, arrange a second date, ideally with the same safety rules. Use the time in between for further e-mails or telephone conversations. Love can also happen at second sight. If it doesn't, tell the person honestly. That also goes the other way around: you may be hooked right from the start, but the other person doesn't necessarily feel the same way. Don't shower him or her with declarations of love or worse, wedding plans. People who are seriously seeking a partner should allow themselves time to sound each other out and size each other up.

- *Start fresh.* Resist the temptation to open yourself up to the other person by pouring out your heart. By the same token, wailing about your ex or tearing apart your previous partners on the first date will also probably scare that person off. If you (or the other person) feel the need to unload like this, then you're probably still hung up on your last relationship, and the new one won't have much of a chance. A good rule of thumb: only when you can think calmly of your ex-partner and are no longer pining after someone is it time to start a new relationship.
- *Formulate your rejections with style.* If you meet someone and realize that the chemistry isn't right, don't just turn that person away without a word. Thank the person for the date, and tell him or her in a friendly way that you aren't interested in having further contact. You don't need to go into detail; just

say honestly: "I don't feel like we fit together." Before you give any concrete feedback, ask the other person if he or she would like to hear it. Some people receive feedback negatively. Many are seriously interested in hearing it, though, and use it to alter their approach next time (if, for instance, they have a tendency to interrupt or nervously fiddle with car keys). This feedback shouldn't be a slap in the face, but a friendly parting gesture.

■ *Don't worry.* Realistically, it's unlikely that you will find a new life partner among your first few contacts. Don't give up after the first letdown—keep trying again at regular intervals. Here is a tip for simplification: treat it like a game or an adventure. You gain self-confidence through your partner search, and you practice your social skills. Even if you don't find your true love, you might make a few new friends.

Finding a Partner Through Personal Ads. TV moderator Petra Gerster met her husband, journalist Christian Nürnberger, through a personal ad in the newspaper *Die Zeit.* The good old personal ad is currently experiencing an unexpected boom in the Internet age. If long e-mail correspondence isn't your thing, and you prefer proper letters, you should give a newspaper personal ad a try. Here are a few tips for composing and answering ads.

■ *Choose the right paper.* A local paper puts you in touch with people who have close ties to home, while a regional, cultural, or economic journal reaches other target groups. For young singles, there are the weekly culture magazines of the larger cities. It's a good idea to read the paper for a few weeks to test it out, and study the personal ads: do you feel as if the overall style speaks to you? Beware of ads with pictures; they almost always lead you to services that charge money!

- *Provide information, not clichés.* Don't brag about yourself in your ad; rather, approach it as a friendly business card with a fitting message. It should reflect your personality and speak to like-minded people. Simplifying tip: think of a real person you've had a crush on (probably someone who's unfortunately already taken). What could you write that would catch that person's interest? Avoid empty phrases: don't be another guy looking for a woman "who looks great, whether in jeans or in an evening gown." Forget the long lists of adjectives: who wouldn't claim to be loving, intelligent, honest, and loyal? Your approach to life is much more interesting: Do you want children? Are you a bookworm or a computer geek? An athlete or a couch potato? A homebody or a travel bug?

- *Don't be stingy.* Ads do cost money. Business-minded men in particular tend to want to save space; so they put one puzzling abbreviation after another into their ads. But you're probably not looking for a person who likes to decipher hieroglyphs— you want a romantic partner! If your budget is really so tight, it's better to leave a few words out altogether, and spell the rest out completely.

- *What to do with the responses?* If you've put some personality into your ad, you can expect a personal reply. That means you can throw out form letters that say nothing specific, as well as hastily scribbled notes. Only answer the letters that directly refer to the text of your ad. If you receive no letters or very few, don't take it too hard. Place another ad very soon (with a new text or in a different newspaper).

- *How do you answer an ad?* The most important thing is to write why precisely this ad spoke to you. Don't give the impression that you're answering a hundred personal ads a week with a standard letter. Write one or two pages—it should

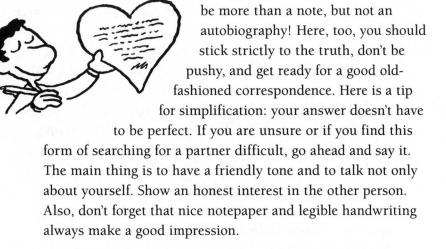

be more than a note, but not an autobiography! Here, too, you should stick strictly to the truth, don't be pushy, and get ready for a good old-fashioned correspondence. Here is a tip for simplification: your answer doesn't have to be perfect. If you are unsure or if you find this form of searching for a partner difficult, go ahead and say it. The main thing is to have a friendly tone and to talk not only about yourself. Show an honest interest in the other person. Also, don't forget that nice notepaper and legible handwriting always make a good impression.

Simplifying Idea 7: Learn to Flirt— the Art of Building Your Tent

When you're interested in another person, whether at work, in your Spanish class, or on an Internet date, the real challenge begins: can the two of you put up a love tent together? For simplicity's sake, we call this the art of flirting. The origin of this word is the Latin flora for flower. In French, the word fleuretir is derived from the Latin, meaning to surround someone with flowers. The essential meaning of flirt is already there in the French word: creating a pleasant mood with a cheerful air and making convincing compliments.

Flirting for Beginners

Two examples of flirting attempts gone awry:

He: "Wow, is it full here or what?"

She: "If you would just get out of here, there would be some more room!"

Or the opposite,

She: "Pretty loud here, huh?"

He: "Then why not just keep your mouth shut?"

Even when the snub is less harsh, this kind of thing hurts. When the love tent collapses the first time you try to put it up, it makes you feel insecure. So we're offering you a little refresher course in flirting to help you overcome your fear of the brush-off. First, we offer a few points to think about; then comes the practice.

Lighten Up. Let go of the notion that a flirtation has to lead to sex, love, or a long-term relationship. The "scattering flowers" of flirting is in the first place an art that every man and woman should practice. Resolve to develop your own flirting style. Become a person who likes to interact with others. Practice the craft of tent building by putting up little canopies that have nothing to do with love and romance. Then you will loosen up yourself and those around you.

Count on Seeing and Being Seen. Psychologist Dorothy Tennov studied the diaries of people in love as part of her research on how love begins. She discovered one consistently effective trigger of attraction: the feeling of being desired. Tennov's conclusion was that "desire awakens when you feel that you are desired." So you need to awaken that desire in the other person.

This is the real purpose of flirting: to find out as much as possible about whether the external attraction also corresponds to an inner one.

Be Truly Stimulating. With the right know-how, you can considerably increase the probability of a successful flirtation. The best scientifically proven flirtation enhancers are movement and curiosity.

- *A strong heartbeat intensifies emotions.* Exercise is an intensifier for men because the heart rate is linked to physical tension. A strong heartbeat is an indication of excitement and alertness, giving a man the tense awareness of a Stone Age hunter. More can come of flirting when men dance to music with strong bass tones in the rhythm of a heartbeat, than when they dance with music that doesn't have that heartbeat.

Simplifying Tip for Women: Take advantage of situations in which physical exertion makes a man's heart beat faster and stronger. In the best-case scenario, such a situation is tied to a promising ambiguity about you, which places him in even more tension. In plain English, you show that you're open to him but haven't yet decided for sure—so he still has to chase you. ■

■ *Curiosity intensifies affection.* Women feel good not only when they are admired for their looks, but also when they sense that there's more behind this admiration. The famed ladies' man and writer Giacomo Casanova said it best: "Love is two-thirds curiosity."

Simplifying Tip for Men: Show the woman not only that you find her beautiful, but also that you're even more fascinated by what you see of her personality. A man's curiosity for a woman's inner person is the real hit with women. Give a woman your whole attention, and take note of her opinions. Hold back a little so that you don't come off as too intrusive. When a woman first meets a man, she wants to see a hero with all kinds of possibilities, one of which might be a romantic future together. If she doesn't see this and is looking for a serious relationship, she will write him off as a guy just looking for an affair. ■

The Four Phases of Flirtation

Anthropologist David Givens and biologist Timothy Perper researched flirting behavior for several years in bars, cafés, nightclubs, and other typical meeting places. Their conclusion was that the construction of a love tent proceeds according to a secret pattern with surprisingly consistent rules that flirting partners obey as their instruction manual. The most important ground rule is that the woman determines the speed of the tent's construction, but the man distinguishes himself as the more confident tent builder.

Building Your Tent, Phase 1: Eye Contact. In flirting, the woman is the director. She decides whether and when something happens or doesn't. If she looks at him and also smiles at him, then a man will be brave approaching her. But most men keep their distance if the woman doesn't waste a glance on them.

Flirt researcher Monica Moore of Webster University in St. Louis, Missouri, has shown that even if men want good-looking women, a particular woman's looks alone don't determine whether she attracts men. In the end, the deciding factor is the number of flirtation signals that she sends out.

> **Simplifying Tip for Women:** It's not just about how you look, but how you look *at* a man. When you go out, don't surround yourself the whole time with a cluster of girlfriends or other conversation partners. This makes it hard for a man to exchange flirt signals with you. Make sure that a man can get you alone and talk to you. Take a hint from the classical flirting repertory: looks, smiles, tilting your head, running your fingers through your hair, and tossing your head back (the "hair flip"). The more of these signals you send out, the higher the chances that a man will react. But be careful: as soon as definite eye contact occurs, negative signals will no longer be taken seriously by most men. In this case, you must express your disinterest very unambiguously. You don't have to be hurtful, even if you have to repeat a firm dismissal: this man is looking for love just like you and should be able to pull away without losing face. ◼

> **Simplifying Tip for Men:** Women standing alone often unconsciously send out "nonspecific" flirt signals. So you shouldn't assume at the first eye contact that such a woman is interested

in you. Even if she's in the mood to flirt, it's possible that she didn't even remotely mean for you to approach her. To test whether those flirt signals are really meant for you, stand in a different part of the room. If she tracks you with her eyes or goes so far as to turn toward you, you may proceed—the flirting game has begun. If on the other hand, she clearly rebuffs you, you absolutely must respect it. Make a charming remark as you depart ("I would have always regretted it if I hadn't at least tried." or "Too bad, but I respect that, of course. Nice talking to you!") and withdraw. This way, you're not slinking away a loser—you've ended the conversation yourself. It's always worthwhile to remain friendly with a woman. Maybe the right one for you will pop up in the form of her best friend. In that case, it would be doubly bad luck if the first thing her friend heard was how this pushy guy just wouldn't get lost. ■

Building Your Tent, Phase 2: The First Sentence. What should a man say to a woman? Sociologist Kate Fox of Oxford has found that when a man flirts with a woman, the first sentence doesn't have to be anything special. The more harmless and noncommittal you begin, the better. Imagine that you're "just" making conversation. Women prefer an approach without obvious intentions. They only accept direct come-on lines when it's done in a graceful or charming way ("Excuse me if I just pop up like this, but I can't help myself—I just had to talk to you."). The safest thing is for men to avoid altogether those cocky, macho lines that come on too directly and crudely.

When a woman wants to say something first, there's good news: men hardly care at all how a woman approaches them. You can say something nice, harmless, or even sassy—the main thing is that *you* are starting the conversation. But be careful: once you have taken the initiative, you don't get out of the situation so easily. When your assertive behavior is so unambiguous, a man becomes more convinced of your intentions the more you talk with him.

Building Your Tent, Phase 3: Delicate Bonds. A strict ground rule is that in flirting, nearness is created through words and looks, not through hands. It's also about holding a conversation. As long as the two of you don't run out of things to talk about, you're weaving the fabric that can one day become the walls of your love tent. Phase three is there to make as many of these delicate bonds as possible. First with words and then—very slowly—also through "accidental" touches.

Simplifying Tip: In an effort to cover up their own insecurity and keep the flirtatious conversation going, most people talk too much about themselves. This mistake is especially common among men. They end up giving the impression that they're self-obsessed and aren't really concerned about the person sitting across from them. When you're flirting, the cardinal rule is that you don't have to be *interesting*. You have to be *interested*. And that means interested in this concrete person!

A good balance is to talk a third of the time and listen for two-thirds, so you can be really focused on the other person. Ask questions and show interest in what the other person does or thinks. Get to know the person's likes and dislikes, and show that you're curious: "That's interesting, what you just said . . . and how do you like . . . what do you think of . . . do you like to . . . have you ever . . . " You don't want this to be an interrogation, though—it shouldn't feel like you're pumping the person for information! If the other person asks you something, make your answer refer back to him or her: "I'm sure that something so dumb wouldn't ever happen to you like it did to me . . . ."

Also, reduce the volume of the conversation. It's hard for the magic to work if you're having to yell at each other over a loud party, in a full club, or at a noisy bar. It's better to flirt in places where you can gradually speak more softly so that the person across from you has to lean a little bit closer to hear you. If your listener doesn't find this unpleasant, he or she will remain in this position, screening the two of you off from other people. Your conversation takes on a private and intimate character.

If this strategy is successful, you can move on to the next level. The trick to this, though, is not to crowd the other person.

Timing is everything! If you break through the invisible intimacy boundary too early, the other person will reflexively pull back, and you'll have lost that opportunity. Physical contact is risky. During this phase, the most that's allowed is to "accidentally" brush or otherwise minimally touch the other person. Afterward, you must immediately pull back. The waist, the hips, and especially the behind are all off-limits; grabbing is completely forbidden. Eros may tantalizingly flicker between you, but he can't be allowed to just shove Amor aside. ■

Simplifying Tip: Whisper something in the other person's ear, and then sit back again. This is a good opportunity for establishing contact that is intimate but still appropriate. When you're that close, though, you shouldn't be whispering something romantic or erotic—that would be overdoing it. It's better to combine this exciting push into the other's intimate space with a harmless, witty confession that makes the other person laugh: "I've never told a woman this before, but I love Jane Austen (or "Days of Our Lives," teddy bears, Shirley Temples, sandwiches with the crusts cut off, etc.)! But this is just between us, OK?"

The true art of flirting is in catching just the right moment. If you hesitate too long, the right opportunity passes by quickly. If you go too fast and force things, you irritate the other person. Here is a good rule: a flirtation is a promise, not its fulfillment. Thoughtful compliments will take you further than heated declarations of love—but they must fit the individual and not sound trite. Don't restrict yourself to just complimenting a person's appearance. The more attention you pay to the other person's personality, the more easily you will recognize his or her inner virtues. When you discover one of them, let the person know! ■

Building Your Tent, Phase 4: The Body Echo. You recognize the fourth phase of flirting by the way your and the other person's movements begin to harmonize with each other, unconsciously resonating with one another. Your mutual interest registers in the harmony of your behavior. The more in tune you feel, the stronger the seduction. When bodies communicate on the same wavelength, both people show that they feel comfortable with each other and could get used to each other. When you've reached this level, Eros has free reign—even if the other person is still a complete stranger.

> **Simplifying Tip:** Skillful seduction has something playful about it from the start. The same goes for the first kiss. When you think the right moment has come, but you're uncertain if the other is ready, just ask in a soft voice: "What would you say if I kissed you right now?" and wait for a minute. This creates much more erotic tension than a wordless kiss! Also, the other person can still say no before you actually do anything. ▓

Don't Disconnect Eros from Amor

But do keep them separate! The secret rule behind flirting says that lovers have a better chance for long-term happiness together the more alike they are. In the fourth phase of flirtation, this is realized on the physical level. Differences disappear when passionate attraction is present. Eros sees to that. You can leave it at that or also use this process as a model for Amor, because something spiritual also that corresponds to that body echo.

A study at Harvard University has shown that long-term couples achieve this resonating effect on all other levels. Rather than growing apart over time, they adjusted themselves to each other. This was easier to achieve the more alike they were. The ideal long-term partner is someone who feels familiar to you from the beginning. Psychologist and science journalist Bas Kast has compared hundreds of studies on couples and concludes the following: people who are similar understand each other better; validate each other; and have similar worldviews, values, and goals. "In the rush of passion we don't see these goals. But over the course of a relationship they become crucial." All serious matchmaking agencies are founded on this insight.

Here is a simplification tip for everyone who is looking for a stable relationship: when flirting you have to learn to play the long shots, just like when you're playing pool. Try to use so much skill and patience that you can clearly hear Amor's spirit echo before Eros's body echo overwhelms you.

Simplifying Idea 8: Refine the Art of Pleasure

The fact that it's an ever-present topic in the media would make you think that it's obvious what "sex" is. But it isn't obvious. Is it purely the act of sexual intercourse, which on average lasts eleven minutes (a fact that inspired the title of a book by Paul Coelho)? Or is every encounter between lovers "sex"? We think that we've found a good clue to the answer.

Clarify What Sex Actually Is

"And Adam knew his wife Eve." In the Old Testament, the idea of "knowing" someone was used to refer to sexual intercourse. *Yada'h* (the apostrophe stands for a glottal stop) is the Hebrew word for this "knowing" and is reminiscent of the primal call "Yes! There!" This is everyone's deepest wish: to be known by another person for who you are in your innermost being. This begins when the two of you are naked together and show each other everything that no one is normally allowed to see. You touch each other in places where no one else may touch you. You experience physical sensations and ecstatic moments that you could only experience together.

The catch to all of this, though, is that you also encounter each other in a completely defenseless and exposed state. Humans have a great advantage over all other mammals in that we can face each other during sexual intercourse. This insight into the deeper nature of sexuality leads us to what may be the most important piece of simplifying advice on the topic of sex: be honest.

The Best Aphrodisiac. Because sex is the most radical form of mutual acknowledgment, honesty is the strongest potion for better sex. If you lie to your lover, he or she will soon lose sexual interest in you. That goes for both small and large falsehoods—not only sexual unfaithfulness, but also unexpressed feelings, hidden injuries, and bottled-up anger. Lies in every form bring sexual feelings out of synch and can even make them run dry.

On the other hand, the most effective treatment for sexual problems is speaking the truth. Often, these are truths that you don't want to burden your partner with, things you're ashamed of, or things that you've repressed, sometimes even to the point of completely forgetting them. In these cases, you should seek professional help to work through these emotional barriers, and help is possible.

If you find that your sexual feelings for your partner are fading or disappear altogether, look around for anything that you may be hiding or keeping silent. As soon as you discuss this openly with your partner, your good vibrations will return with renewed energy.

Knowing also has something to do with *acknowledging*. If one of you has the feeling that you're no longer being acknowledged by the other, Eros hits the off switch.

The Great Taboo. Sometimes we feel like we're living in an age without taboos where no ideas are off-limits. But with every taboo broken, some other area becomes a forbidden zone. In the case of sex, the unspoken yet indisputable fact is that it's there to bring new life into the world. Sex and children go together. Sexual desire draws its tremendous energy and dynamism from this. The medical sciences pride themselves on having separated desire and reproduction through the pill and other effective methods of contraception. However, spiritual

 institutions remind us again and again that the two actually belong together. The pope does this for the Catholic Church, while the Dalai Lama does it for Buddhism; all forms of Islam and Hinduism do it as well.

Couples who have sex to create a child speak of a totally different dimension of sex. Erotic activity where a life is created or could be created is of a different quality than sex with pills and condoms. A man who fathers a child and a woman who conceives a child are ancient archetypes that are rooted deep within each person and have an undeniable power. This doesn't mean that sex without the intent to conceive a child is bad or that a childless couple is worth less than couples with children. But when considering the primal energies within us, you shouldn't forget this basic truth: in every sexual encounter lies the unspoken question: "Do we want to have a child together?" Is there anything more intimate, more intense than this?

Follow the Rules of the Erotic Conversation

It is particularly beautiful with your partner in the love tent if you know the art of erotic communication. Ninety percent of all sexual problems are communication problems: nearly all professional counselors agree on this. On the other hand, talking about erotic moments is an especially touchy thing, even among our most sexually liberal contemporaries. This is because it touches upon the highly sensitive area of erotic pride. When you talk about sex, the key question usually is, how can you enhance your own sexual self-awareness and that of your partner without weakening—or worse—destroying it?

In his book *Erotic Intelligence*, psychoanalyst and sex therapist Jack Morin has formulated ten rules of erotic communication based on his decades of professional experience. Actually, there are three absolute don'ts and seven tips, a few of which you'll intuitively take to heart. You should note the ones that you've already come across without knowing it and mentally paint them on the inner walls of your love tent. They are incredibly important!

Three Don'ts for Talking About Intimacy. It's easy to destroy an intimate relationship or to put up a block in your relationship that lingers for years. Imagine that three large warning signs are hanging at the entrance of your love tent:

1. *Never put your partner down sexually.* Insults and attacks that belittle, degrade, or disrespect your partner sexually have a devastating effect on the relationship. These things can't be undone. Damage at this level goes deep and remains there forever. Sexual insults can mean the end of your sex life together or even the end of the entire relationship.

2. *Never compare your partner with your past lovers.* This is a surefire relationship killer. When you do this, you are being unkind to both your former lover and your current partner because you are demonstrating that you don't know how to acknowledge, appreciate, and protect the intimacy of a relationship. Then open, unself-conscious sexuality becomes out of the question.

3. *Never complain to a friend or relative about your sex life and the sexual shortcomings of your partner.* Again, here you damage the intimate sphere that you share. First, you put that outside third party in an uncomfortable position, and second, you can bet that your complaints will be repeated—usually in a distorted form or with negative commentary. Even your best friend shouldn't be the complaint box for your sex life. If you need advice, turn to someone "neutral," who is outside of your life. This *don't* applies especially and with many exclamation points to conversations with your children. It doesn't matter how old or intelligent your

children are, or how great your need is: don't discuss your sex life with your children—ever!

Seven Tips for Talking About Intimacy

1. *Give your partner regular positive feedback, verbal and nonverbal.* If there's something that you especially like, tell your partner. It's good to tell your partner what you like, but it's even better to also take your partner's hand and show him or her. Best of all is acknowledging your partner when he or she does what you like (e.g., "Yes, that's it, *that* feels good"). With these positive encouragements, you build up a strong bond and a lot of trust.

2. *Only talk about sexual problems and dissatisfactions when you are close.* And not when one of you is tired, irritated, annoyed, frustrated, or preoccupied. Always make sure that both of you associate your conversations about sex with comfortable situations. The best opportunity is usually right after a satisfying time in bed together.

3. *If you are uncomfortable speaking directly about sex, write a letter first.* This way, you can choose your words carefully, and your partner has time to think it over. End the letter with the request that the two of you talk about the issues you brought up. If you use the five-ribbon trick for writing love letters (discussed later in this chapter), you will be able to come up with the right words to express your deep affection while broaching the topic of sex. In such a letter, be sure to express your confidence that this will help you understand each other better and learn to love each other more.

4. *In conversations in the love tent, be a particularly good listener.* Don't get defensive. Otherwise, you'll be thinking about your counterarguments the whole time and you won't grasp what your partner wants to tell you. It helps to trade off talking and listening every five minutes.

5. *Ask about the erotic desires and feelings of your partner.* Dare to ask directly. You won't get concrete answers if you ask vague questions. Ask your partner the questions you would like your partner to ask you. Explore together what you like best.

6. *Speak with feeling.* For many women, what really makes them want to have sex is an intense emotional exchange in which she learns something about her partner's deep feelings specifically for her. A rule of thumb for men is to speak twice as emotionally as usual. In their upbringing and their professions, men are taught to be cool. A good rule of thumb for women is to praise him twice as much as you think is normal when he says the right thing to you. Women are used to "giving a little more emotionally" with each other. Feelings are experienced and expressed very differently by the two sexes. When you know this, you keep a low point in your emotional life from becoming a canyon in your sex life.

7. *Learn to be silent.* If in your relationship you are the talker who likes to pepper your partner with questions, it could be useful to trade roles when it comes to sexual questions. Wait during those deciding seconds that you usually fill up with your flood of words (and which may feel like hours of silence to you). Set the tone by bringing up a shared moment that was especially erotic for both of you. Imagine that you are decorating the walls of your love tent with these erotic, lustful images. What would he paint there, and what would she? Come up with lusty memories in which something tender and bonding lights up with Amor. Talk about them with few words, but with the loving conviction that "we can get back to the way it was then." If you do this, you can transform and enchant your partner!

Write Fantastic Love Letters

A love letter doesn't only start off or deepen a relationship. When you court someone in writing, you also become more aware of your own feelings. Let the following tips inspire you to take up your pen again or to send romantic e-mail love notes. Here are a few ground rules for writing love letters that will really get your partner going:

The Only Don't. Your love letter can be crazy or silly, dramatic or somber, stormy or gentle, sassy or shy. You can lament, plead, beg, avow, or adore. There's only one thing you can't do: bore!

The World Revolves Around Your Lover. The topic of a love letter isn't yourself, but the other person. More than half of your thoughts should be exclusively about the person whom you love. Rather than writing grandiose expressions of love, tell the person about what you've experienced with him or her. Don't wail or nag about problem areas in the relationship! Here is a tip for simplification: if you've done something wrong, apologize and take responsibility for it properly. Don't grovel. This makes you unattractive and ruins the equilibrium in a relationship.

The Five-Ribbon Trick. A love letter works when it contains things that bind you to your beloved. We have pulled together five kinds of bonds. Your writing should pick up on at least one of these "ribbons." Don't just write out a bunch of clichés—weave relationship ribbons out of your truly individual thoughts about the other person. If your writing touches on more than one of the ribbons, all the better!

- Love and trust
- Praise and admiration
- Respect and esteem
- Validation and support
- Understanding and sympathy

Of course it's OK to put concerns, doubts, or fears into a love letter. But wrap them up in a warm cushion woven of these five ribbons.

Enhance Your Sexual Desire with the Resonance Effect

The wrong words can really foul up an erotic encounter. That's the bad news. The good news is that with the right words, you can substantially enhance your experience of desire.

Report on What's Going on Inside You. The resonance effect is a technique that gives great results in your sex life—by letting your partner know what he or she is making you feel. Say your partner is stroking your thigh, and it feels good. "Do that again" is often what you would say, but this is a command that may provoke negative feelings in your partner, even if you didn't mean it that way. The resonance method is smarter: you say how that touch makes you feel: "When you touch me like that, I get these amazing shivers all over my body." When you're feeling sexually excited and you let your partner know, this excitement is increased for both of you! "Wow, that really turns me on," is one of the most effective resonance lines (assuming that it's really the truth).

Trust the Erotic Feedback Effect. Communicating your feelings this way takes practice. But the resonance effect works even when you haven't quite mastered it yet. Here are a few more ideas: "When I look into your eyes, I get all fluttery." "It feels like my blood is singing as it runs through my body." "I think I'm feeling those famous butterflies in my stomach right now." Don't memorize these sentences—listen to your body and then say whatever suits you. Just say something!

When you do this, you set a wonderful cycle in motion: your partner does something and you say how it makes you feel. Then he or she begins to share your feelings and experiences. Your partner doesn't only experience his own feelings when holding, kissing, or stroking you, but experiences your feelings too. You know this and become more excited because the other person is excited by what excites you. This goes on like feedback between a microphone and a speaker until it sings out shrilly. It sounds like and actually is a complex process—but once it gets going, it feels simply delightful.

Enhance Your Sexual Desire Through Touch

It is nice to hug and to feel each other. But with a little practice, you can get a whole lot more out of such familiar touches. Again, it's about the resonance and feedback of feelings. What you just did with words and movements, you can now do with just touches. Try it out first on yourself.

Sensitize Your Body. Hold your hand up in front of you, and concentrate for a while on feeling your fingertips. After a while, you'll start to feel a faint vibration there. For some people this takes longer, but you will feel it eventually. If it's taking too long, rub your fingers briefly against each other and then stretch them out again. Concentrate on different parts of your fingertips, from one finger to the next. You'll notice that you feel a light vibration or prickling right at the spot where you focus your attention—you "switched on" the nerve cells in that particular spot.

Find a spot on your hand that seems especially sensitive to you. For most people, it's the tip of the pointer or middle finger of the right hand. With this finger, touch the wrist of your other hand. As soon as contact is made, you feel a double vibration: in your fingertip and at the spot on your arm that you're touching. After all of this mental preparation, it can tingle so strongly that your wrist actually itches and you have to scratch it. Normally you perceive these kinds of touches all at once, but with a little bit of training beforehand, you feel it doubled: your wrist sends your brain the message "I'm being touched," and your fingertip (in a different way) does too.

The Amazing Nerve Fabric of Love. When you touch your partner, these imaginary yet palpable nerve pathways expand even farther: they go through your lover. That wonderful feeling gets even more intense and stronger; it fills your emotions and can totally overwhelm you.

What starts with breathing, speaking, and touching can end in an all-encompassing resonance of your two beings. Far too many people settle for an unthinking coexistence and unself-conscious sex. Conscious sensations, conscious feedback of your own inner experiences with those of the other person, and the conscious eroticism that goes along with it is new for many people. But once you've begun to discover the true potential of your sexuality, you'll never go back to those (comparatively) meager sensations you had before.

Pay Attention to the Superficial Things

In *How to Simplify Your Love*, simplifying always means getting rid of whatever is unnecessary or in the way so there's room for what actually counts. That goes especially for physical love, because blocks in this area are especially problematic and can make sex difficult or even impossible—sometimes for a long time.

The following pieces of advice will seem so obvious that they may make you smile. But it happens again and again that liaisons that start out so promisingly fail because of some ridiculous little detail.

Think About Your Hygiene. We have concluded that this is the number one culprit in relationships that never got off the ground or that had intimacy problems: someone has bad breath, greasy hair, or something else about his or her appearance that is off-putting. Let's tell it like it is: usually, it's the man. Tragically, that person usually has no idea, and apparently either no one dares to tell him or he's a believer in that backward logic that says, "That kind of thing doesn't really matter." But it *does* matter! Our advice for simplification: find a person who will act as your "living mirror" and who is allowed to say absolutely anything about your appearance. If at all possible, this should not be a relative or anyone who is in some way dependent on you, since these people might not have the heart to be direct or will be too careful.

If you can't find anyone in your circle of friends or acquaintances, go to a professional. Talk to your dentist. He not only knows something about bad breath, he also knows what to do about it. If you're afraid of the dentist and haven't been to one in a long time, then there's a pretty good chance that your breath is driving away potential partners—even if you are otherwise a wonderful person.

Another good adviser in these matters is your hairdresser. Or a dermatologist or a beautician—you would be amazed how many people will help you look and feel more attractive. You can gain so much confidence from the experience!

Don't Underestimate AIDS. Over the past twenty years or so, acquired immunodeficiency syndrome (AIDS) has completely transformed people's sex lives. It is passed through the human immunodeficiency virus (HIV), and the infection numbers have been rising. So we're warning you: when you have sex with another person, the danger of HIV infection is not negligible. You can't tell from looking at a person whether he or she is infected. A person also can be infected and not know it yet.

There is no cure for AIDS, despite all the progress that has been made in this direction. New treatments make it easier to live with the illness, but those infected with HIV must live with the risk of severe side effects.

HIV can be contracted when a bodily fluid containing a sufficiently large amount of the virus enters another body. The key bodily fluids in HIV infection are semen, vaginal fluids, and blood, even in small amounts. HIV is not contracted through everyday contact, such as sneezing, working in a hospital, or going in saunas or swimming pools, but it can be transmitted through any kind of unprotected sexual activity (e.g., vaginal, anal, and oral), or any contact with blood (e.g., injections, transfusions, fights, injuries, accidents).

Talk this issue over with your partner—your life is worth it. This is not the time for false modesty! Being concerned about safe sex does not express mistrust, but rather shows your sense of responsibility. Tell your partner, "I want us both to protect ourselves." To be on the safe side, both men and women should carry condoms with them, even if a sexual encounter seems only very distantly possible!

Clean out Your Bedroom. One of the most successful basic ideas in *How to Simplify Your Life* was that when you're feeling blocked, you should first try clearing away the heaps and piles in your home.

Anything that's just lying around, waiting to be fixed or taken care of, is a symbol for the clutter inside of you. Many people think that they have to start with their souls and become a new person before they can really clean up their room. But it also works the other way around: cleaning up is liberating! That goes for the love tent, as well.

What kind of space you celebrate your togetherness in makes a difference. In those first heated encounters, it might not be your biggest concern, but over time it can really matter whether you make love between mountains of dirty laundry or in a place where the two of you are happy to wake up together in. Store as little as possible under the bed. When you're lying in bed, you should not have broken objects or unfinished projects staring at you. Here is a simplifying tip for a last-minute cleanup with the maximum effect: clear the floor and at least one other surface, so the chaos doesn't seem as overwhelming.

Another very important element is lighting. Make sure you have low but friendly lighting that doesn't blind you. If you want candlelight, make sure that the candles are on a sturdy surface. If you want to have music, it should only be music that both partners like and fades easily into the background. Otherwise, silence is much nicer and more erotic.

Simplifying Idea 9:
Safeguard Your Love Tent

Unfortunately, there's always the chance that your love won't be returned. You secretly fall in love and set up a wonderful tent in your heart for your beloved; then reality steps in and you don't become a couple. Your hopes and dreams burst like soap bubbles. You realize it but don't say a word, and you suffer in silence. Maybe a promising romance even did get started; then the fragile tent collapsed. You had your hopes up, but now you're suddenly being ignored, rejected, or mercilessly dismissed. Or perhaps you ended the relationship yourself, though it broke your heart to do it.

First Aid for a Broken Heart

No matter what kind of heartbreak you're going through, it hurts terribly. Your feelings are still there, even if they're not returned. There's no magic spell to heal a broken heart, but here are a few tried-and-true tips for easing heartaches big and small, and for preserving your faith in love.

Take Care of Yourself.

- *Indulge in physical relaxation.* This includes sitting in a sauna, swimming, jogging, getting a massage, and taking a bath. Soothing relaxation also harmonizes a bruised soul and an exhausted spirit. Heed the wise words of poet Sylvia Plath: "There must be quite a few things a hot bath won't cure, but I

don't know many of them." Focus on the advantages of being single again: What is easier now? In what ways are you less restricted? What have you always liked to do? Do the things that always annoyed your ex. If you had given up something because of him or her, now you have the freedom to take it up again. Enjoy doing the things you like whenever you want. But be sure to avoid the places that you used to go together, as they are now filled with memories.

- *Stay away from alcohol.* Men in particular tend to "drown" their heartache so they don't have to feel that pain anymore. But if you repress the pain, you'll be struggling longer with the depressive moods, fear of failure, and feelings of guilt that it causes. You're better off confronting the pain and saying to its face: "I can get through this. My heart is greater and stronger than this pain. Another woman will know how to appreciate me."

- *Avoid nervous eating.* This false comfort is extremely common among women. But you can't satisfy your hunger for love this way. Your body can handle that first chocolate attack, but if this becomes a regular occurrence, you program yourself to expect this substitute satisfaction and grab something to eat every time you're upset. If you fall into the other extreme, and your heartache attacks your stomach so much that you can't eat anything, you should at least make sure that you're getting enough vitamins.

- *Get active.* Move your body. Walk. Exercise. If you're depressed, it gives you an energy boost. If you're boiling with rage, it offers you a safe and effective outlet. Exercise helps your body to produce the mood-stimulators that you desperately need.

  Get yourself a new haircut or a new outfit. The external change helps you look at yourself from a different angle and redefine yourself. So in your everyday life, put some effort into your appearance, even if you're a man. This helps you strengthen your sense of self, and you'll get an extra boost from the looks you get from the opposite sex!

- *Take a break from love.* Don't make yourself too available to your ex. This only drives your self-esteem further into the toilet. Don't call, don't send messages, and don't get together "just to clear some things up."

  Be careful about jumping into another relationship. If you go looking for comfort in another lover, then you're using the new person as a consolation. In the end, this just hurts the both of you and starts the whole cycle over again. Instead, pull back into your tower for a little while. Now is when you need it the most!

Right Now, You Need Friends.

■ *No malicious gossiping.* Ask your mutual friends not to try to act as go-betweens between the two of you. For women, your best friend is usually the best person to comfort you. Have a good cry so your anger and sadness don't eat away at you. But both sexes should keep in mind the following: don't talk badly about your ex, and don't let others do it, either. The more you disparage your ex, the more negatively you will later have to judge your own relationship capability: How could *you* (with your perfect intuition) get involved with such a jerk? How could *you* (with your clever head) fall for such a witch? You'll notice how much simpler your love life is when you firmly state, "We are both decent people, but we just didn't fit together."

■ *No romanticizing.* On the other hand, avoid idealizing your ex. Don't cling to your memories of happy times together or hold on to photos that bring a new flood of tears every time you look at them. Gather up all of the pictures and reminders of your relationship, pack everything into a box, and banish them to the attic or the cellar.

■ *No embarrassing scenes.* If you still have a few of your partner's belongings at your place (or vice versa), ask a friend to bring them over. If the things are too heavy and have to be picked up, you should set up a time when this can be done. Make sure that you are not alone at home when this takes place. The best protection against a surge of confusing emotions is having friends with you who make you feel calm and secure.

■ *No taking sides.* Don't ask your friends to decide whose side they're on. These loyalties will work themselves out gradually on their own. Generally, your ex's friends stay your ex's friends and yours stay yours.

Invent a Parting Ritual.

- *Reevaluate through writing.* The act of writing creates distance from your experiences. What strengths and weaknesses did you and your partner show in your relationship? What mistakes did your partner make? How did you contribute to the failure of the relationship?

- *A farewell fire.* A particularly effective parting ritual is to write a letter of farewell where you can pour out your grief without restraint. Don't send this letter, though, and don't hold on to it either; rather, burn it as a symbol of letting go.

- *A place of power.* Find a "pilgrimage site" for your symbolic farewell. This can be a church, a secluded mountain, a park bench under a shady tree, a stretch of harbor, or even a special café. Just as you visited certain places with your ex, which are now loaded with memories, let this new site rejuvenate you with energy for a new beginning. This way, you can tell yourself later: "We sat in that courtyard so often. But here in the rose garden by the lake, I started my new life."

- *Get closure.* Attempting to stay friends usually doesn't work. There's almost always a certain imbalance, because so often one person has a lingering, unconscious desire to win the other person back. Spare yourself that pressured feeling or that guilty conscience. Friendly relations usually only come after a period of clear distance, during which both parties can let go of their injuries.

Discover the 70 Percent Secret

Nothing and no one can suppress love. Like a tornado, passion sweeps through the hearts of people in love. This is the central theme of the novels of the Japanese author Haruki Murakami. He has his own Eastern view of love, which can be especially helpful after the end of a relationship. His insight is that the perfection of love lies in its acceptance of the lovers' imperfection.

Allow Each His or Her Own Inner World. In Eastern thought, loving someone doesn't mean completely giving up your own complex inner life—you can't ask that of your partner, either. Loving someone, in Eastern cultures, means respecting the mysterious inner world of your partner without being able to know it completely. This Eastern knowledge is spreading into other continents (through the globalization of culture).

Let Go of Your Ideals of Perfection. People from yes-or-no cultures like ours often dream of a partner who is 100 percent perfect for them. They live with the unconscious expectation that their current 80 percent partner will someday be followed by a 90 percent one, and then, hopefully, by a 100 percent one. They seek the perfect man or the perfect woman, and when they don't find that person, they get divorced and then remarry, only to discover again that they still haven't found their 100 percent partner. "In Japan we fundamentally assume that there is no perfect love. We seek the person who fits in 70 percent and then fill the rest in ourselves." This 30 percent is the shared creation of a couple. This 30 percent represents the actual treasure of your relationship. Look at it in comparison with politics: if a political party had a 70 percent majority, it would rule and shape its country almost single-handedly.

The idea of 100 percent harmony has one more hitch: if there actually were to be such an accord between two people, neither of them would be able to change. The relationship would be cursed from the start, a perfect picture frozen in eternity. Nothing would be able to move or shift. Every change would be an attack on the relationship. You can be glad that it's not ever like this. A living, loving, relationship is not a static state of being, but rather a dynamic becoming.

The following line comes from German actor and director Curt Goetz: "How did I meet my wife? By marrying her." Love is both a wonderful and a trying path to maturity, upon which two 70 percent people create a

100 percent work of art: their relationship. In the process, they come to know each other more deeply than they knew themselves before. They continually shape, remodel, and create something new. Mature couples know that they are not perfect, and they don't want to be. The real greatness is the understanding between them. "It's not the end of the world," Murakami explained with a smile during an interview, "but you have to plunge deep into yourself in order to grasp it."

The Third Dwelling of Love
The Homestead

Your Simplifying Dream: The Homestead

The sun rises. The long, exquisitely warm and sweet night is over. This is a wonderful moment of awakening, these minutes between dream and reality in which you try to orient yourself . . . you lie in a soft bed, but you're no longer in a tent. You no longer feel the wind nor hear the sounds of nature. Above you is a wooden ceiling with sturdy beams, in front of you a window through which the morning sun is shining. You get up, feel the wood floor under your feet, and see a room painted in a friendly yellow. In the bed, your love is still sleeping. But where are you?

You go to the window and squint out into the sunlight. A sparrow flutters by, and you look upon a grand garden with open fields stretching out beyond it. Off in the distance a horse and carriage drive by. You're upstairs in what seems to be quite a large house. With each breath, you remember more clearly: you know this house; you belong here. You open the door and go down a sweeping staircase into a great hall. The broad front doors are standing open. In front of the house are a bench and a blooming garden. Farther away is a large building—a stable or a barn. Your gaze falls on the kitchen: the table is set the way you prepared it yesterday. You remember how yesterday you both worked here until the evening, and today you'll continue.

As you climb the stairs, you notice two feelings inside of you: one is the wish to keep dreaming into the day. The other is the desire to go forward with yesterday's work. Your love is already in the shower singing. You brush your hand over the banister and suddenly feel very proud. Everything that you see, smell, and feel here is what the two of you have built together. A cheerful strength wells up inside of you. You look forward to the day and begin to chime in with the little song coming out of the bathroom: "Lovers don't finally find each other somewhere; they're in each other all along . . . "

We call this part of your journey through the kingdom of love the *homestead*. Here you work and live together; here both lovers can build a stable future together. Here you create something lasting and contribute to society and the world. On the homestead, there is always something to be done, take care of, consider, provide for, and nourish. Multiple responsibilities demand your time, and stress impacts both of you: stress about finances, career, health, and other people. How does a couple in love endure all this?

An ever-growing number of couples don't manage this transition. Especially striking examples occur among Hollywood stars, whose films almost always take place in the love tent and who apparently believe that the world outside should function in a similar way. They are shocked to find that in real life, those feverish, infatuated encounters aren't followed by the next love scene, but by everyday life. They marry, quarrel, divorce, marry, quarrel . . . and so on.

Forever in Love?

We are skeptical whenever wedding guests tell the bride and groom that they hope they are still as in love in ten, twenty, or thirty years as on the first day. In love, yes, but hopefully changed and more experienced

than on that first day. Devoted to each other, yes, but hopefully also more mature and self-confident in their interactions with each other. To us, *How to Simplify Your Love* means freeing yourself from the romantic, shortsighted idea that the infatuation phase of being in love is the ultimate and everything that comes afterward is a step down. Relationships, too, may and must grow up.

From the cuddly perspective of the fluffy cushions in the love tent, the reality of both-feet-on-the-ground everyday life seems dreary and trivial. But this is an illusion. Once you've mastered the homestead, you feel the fine earnestness and the great power that prevail here. When you look back on the rickety love tent, you realize not only how crazy and exhilarating things were there, but also how haphazard and aimless.

You owe your very existence today to people who founded and cultivated a homestead. However it may have looked—a stable childhood, a sheltered childhood, a childhood in an orphanage or one in foster care, and so on—one, two, or even more people made an effort to take care of you and raise you.

Under One Roof

The roof of this homestead symbolizes the new existence that you have come to as a couple: you unite your love under *one* solid roof. The traditional symbol for this is marriage. You create something that binds you together and is greater than either of you alone. Being a couple is the new center of your identity, something you couldn't have without the other person, which is why so many single people are still out there searching for a partner. It's up to you to shape this identity together!

Simplifying Idea 10: Clarify the Marriage Question

In the old days, the veil that the bride wore at her wedding was a promise: the secret of the love tent would not be revealed until the wedding night. Back then, the homestead and love tent were in the same place and were linked through a secure path. Erotic love and celebration of one another were inevitably tied to binding, responsible cohabitation, including the division of labor. It was hard to enjoy the love tent through any other means.

That was then. Today it's much easier to get into the love tent, even multiple times with different partners. In return, though, it's become more difficult to find the path to the homestead and then really stick it out there. The homestead has become the new mystery of love.

Lay a Cornerstone

The transition from your tower to the love tent didn't need a celebration—the infatuation was a festival of its own. The move from the love tent into the homestead, on the other hand, is not always easy. Therefore, it has become tradition to go through a public "rite of passage" to secure the help and the approval of other people. A growing number of couples forgo this ritual, however, for several different reasons:

- Some couples think that their relationship is so private that it's no one's business, not even that of their own families. They perceive themselves in their love tent as something unique, incomparable, and enchanted. They fear that a public commitment and the brouhaha of a family celebration could disturb their intimate love. In the spirit of the romantic ideal, they would rather marry in secret somewhere faraway.
- For others, it seems absurd to demonstrate their love by "signing a piece of paper." Emotions, they say, can't be regulated through a signature.

- Still others are shy and introverted and don't like being the center of attention. They feel uncomfortable having to "parade" their relationship in front of so many eyes.
- Then there are those for whom an "old-fashioned" wedding, with all the financial obligations involved, is simply too expensive.

But for all of these couples, sooner or later the transcendent state of infatuation loses its magic. The couple has to find a way to replace the improvised love tent with a form of togetherness that can stand up to everyday life. This used to happen through public marriage, but that's not necessarily the case anymore. People move in together and try it out first.

Clarify What You Really Want. The result is that people live together in a kind of "waiting period"—a "trial relationship." This is an extremely pragmatic beginning for the couple (they live together and maybe have a child together), but it doesn't necessarily have the following inner conviction, "Sharing my life with you means for me the definitive end of the partner search and the beginning of our life together." The bond between the two of them grows, but neither says how committed they really are. Love binds them together, but the beginning and the reason for this bond isn't named and marked with a clear sign.

Countless men and women spend their best years stuck in this ambiguous in-between state. They often seem powerless and don't know what a boost their relationship would get from making a definite

choice. What could develop quite naturally—a wedding or a marriagelike commitment—just isn't allowed to happen. If you neglect this, you block the path of your own development. Journalist and theologian Horst Keil put it this way: "We're not lacking the strength for dealing with the extraordinary, but with the ordinary."

You're Allowed to Ask for a Decision. At some point, one of the partners will want to marry or make a lasting commitment, while the other one is still hesitating. This is normal. But it's important that you don't just push this question aside. Instead, clarify whether you want to stay together or not—totally independent of how you choose to stay together (as a cohabitating or married couple).

> **Simplifying Tip:** Talk to your partner about the following statement from the great Swiss psychologist C. G. Jung: "Love requires depth and loyalty of feeling, without which love isn't love, but whimsy. True love will always take on lasting, responsible commitments. Love needs freedom to make the choice, but not to carry it out." ∎

Arguments for Getting Married

If both of you say yes to a committed relationship, getting married gives your relationship a very clear status. Clarity is an important feature of a good relationship. Theologian Jörg Zink calls this clear-cut bond "the reliability of the lover for the long haul," which is a good thing that people are meant to have.

Go to the Limit. Your commitment to your beloved also requires that you have the courage to take a risk—one that binds you for the rest of your life. You're merging your life with your partner's, and you trust that this will make your life richer and even more precious. When you say, "I do," you answer a question (perhaps for the first and only time in your life) that encompasses everything. In this question lies not a rigid moral or a coerced desire, but rather an extraordinary source of strength and a strong comfort that carries you through life. In it lies the experience of many generations: a tremendous gain rewards your big gamble.

Overcome Your Fear. Many people are afraid to commit for life. But that fear is itself a bond. The countless failed marriages are the fruits of the fear of losing your freedom. Fear always clouds your vision. In this case, fear of commitment blinds you to the great prize at the end: as a couple, you have the chance to move into a royal palace at the end of your long path together, a palace that you didn't build yourself. It's there waiting for you. The central simplifying message of this book is to see this yes at the beginning while envisioning the palace at the end. Overcome your fear of commitment; look instead at the strength of your love, out of which freedom grows.

Recognize Blocks. When you see young couples in love, you always get the sense that real love wants to be total. "I love you so much that

I want to spend my whole life with you." This isn't external cultural pressure; it's an inner necessity of love.

When one or both partners *don't* want to marry, there's usually an external reason. Often, there's an old attachment to a previous partner or sometimes to parents. Perhaps one person is thinking of unpleasant scenes witnessed in his or her parents' relationship. Children of divorced parents sometimes have difficulty feeling self-sufficient. They prefer to remain unmarried out of love for their parents. The rational reasons they give (e.g., a lower tax bracket, more freedom, higher living costs) are often predominantly superficial and hide a true emotional reason.

Expect a Miracle. People in love experience something miraculous and learn from it that more miracles are waiting for them. Bestselling author John Gray says that a marriage or relationship only has a chance if both people believe in "practical miracles." Happy couples are dreamers and visionaries. They are convinced that the rigid rules of statistics or social scientists don't apply to them. That's the most beautiful simplifying tip for lovers: live as if all your dreams could one day be fulfilled. Develop colorful fantasies of you and your partner understanding and loving each other more day by day, as well as of you continually transforming in wonderful ways.

Arguments for a Lifelong Promise

When despite everything a marriage is out of the question and you want to stay together without having a ceremony, you should take on as many features of a wedding party as possible. Organize a party similar to a wedding, at which you publicly announce your commitment in front of both of your families and friends. If you don't do this, the commitment energy wanes on both sides. Your relationship will be more heavily burdened with the first difficulties.

If that doesn't work for you, you should inform your relatives and friends in writing that the two of you intend to stay together—as formally as possible. Use a letter, not an email or a phone call. Sometimes the decision to become life partners coincides with the birth of a child. In that case, you can use the invitation to a baptism or a birth celebration to announce your commitment. But don't just mention it "by the way"! Making this announcement strengthens all of you: your relationship, your child, and your friends and relatives.

Simplifying Idea 11: Build a Life Together

When a couple moves from the love tent into the homestead, they are, on the one hand, going back to the way that they lived before: back to school or back to work. On the other hand, they are settling a new land: they move in together and unite their households. Oftentimes, this means a change of location for one or the other, and sometimes also a change of workplace. Perhaps one person gives up a career altogether. In any case, there are a lot of details to work out because much changes and a lot of new things take place.

We see this new land as your fields of life, which you plant around your homestead and cultivate. They are there to provide for you and your relationship.

The Classic Two-Field Economy: Career Field and Housework Field

According to this traditional model, the man is the material and social supporter of the family. His income and status determine the social position of the family. The woman is responsible for "the home": the care of possessions, the housework, and the emotional maintenance of the family. In the less common househusband model, this division of labor is reversed, but the result is the same: there is a gap in

the relationship. The person who takes care of the household forgoes something and stands socially and financially beneath the other person. As long as the stay-at-home partner has no problem with this and feels content with it, there's nothing to object to in this time-tested model.

The Family as a Community in Need of Reform. The two-field economy is always a questionable model for the well-educated stay-at-home partner. More and more women and men don't want to view this model as handed down from on high. Studies show that young women and men in particular want to combine work and family. The number of working women continues to increase. Women resist the "automatic" loss of equality that was traditionally required of them once they started a family: with a child comes an inequality with or even dependence on the man. A couple must be able to work creatively against this.

Theoretically, men have long understood the necessity of a fair division of labor in the early phases of family life, but in practice men are often unwilling to make temporary career compromises or cut back on time spent at work for the good of the family. The complaints of women make the men feel unappreciated as breadwinners.

The simplifying solution for this dilemma is to replace the classic two-field-economy and its two separate supporting roles with a more intelligent division of labor.

The Modern Five-Field Economy

With the help of the following model, you can break free from the traditional ideas of your parents and grandparents without losing the advantages they offer of mutual support and reliability. American Ken Wilber, who has researched consciousness, formulated five central interpersonal needs. When they are met, things go well. When they are met in a marriage or partnership, the relationship does well.

Imagine that these five basic needs correspond to five fields around your homestead, which you as a couple cultivate. A good yield from these fields makes up your fortune. A couple is nourished from the fruits of these fields. These fields can also nourish children and even produce an abundance that can support other dependents. The more fields a couple can cultivate and tend together, the richer their relationship—even with all the work it requires.

Shared work in the fields of your homestead nourishes both partners on all five levels. No field belongs to one partner alone. The five-field economy of the couple ideally stretches out even more: your little farmhouse can grow by and by into a magnificent estate.

Always keep in mind that the five dwellings of love are metaphors. A "magnificent estate" doesn't have to mean that you have a large house or a fat bank account. You are prosperous not only when you're a romantic team or a financial partnership, but also when you act as a couple in all areas of your life, when each gradually comes to have a good idea of what the other needs. This way you create a win-win situation in which both of you help yourselves become emotionally, socially, and materially happy.

For each of the five imaginary fields, ask yourself: Do we have this field? Does one of us consider it "his" or "hers," or is it "ours"? How large is this field on our homestead—grand, sufficient, or meager? Is it perhaps a field that is still in the planning stage? It would be great if these descriptions inspire you to plot your homestead according to the five fields.

Field 1: The Wheat Field, or the Material Section. Here, it's about sustenance: shelter, livelihood, career, housework, savings, acquisitions, and the time spent on these things. This field provides for the

material foundations of the couple, the "daily bread" that is symbolized by the "wheat." If you've set a wrong course for your partnership, then this field can produce a lot of stress, where one of you is never satisfied and the other feels deprived because of an insufficient or unjust distribution of rights and duties.

- *The right fertilizer:* You need consistency and fairness in the distribution of internal and external tasks. As the largest field of the homestead, the wheat field requires strategic business management combined with balanced considerations of both landowners' interests. You should be especially fair about dividing your resources of time, money, and energy spent on Field 1.

  Follow a phase-oriented plan, especially if you want to have children or already have them. The child-rearing phase is a narrow bottleneck for your two-sided participation in the job market. The one who primarily cares for the children must have the unconditional support of the other partner in his or her further education and return to work. The one who works and doesn't interrupt a career must make up for it by helping out more at home than before.

■ *The fruits:* When you work as a team, cultivating and shaping your material wheat field, you complete an excellent training for the balance of give and take in the other fields.

That is the revolution—the two fields of the old model are combined into this first field of the modern five-field system. The five-field system believes that material concerns are only part of a relationship. It may be an especially important part, but it's only one-fifth. This first field must be managed in absolute partnership. Possessive pronouns as in "*your* career" or "*my* household" don't exist here. The working partner uses shared resources of time and money just like the person who manages the household.

Field 2: The Garden, or the Emotional Section. Imagine the second field as an aromatic garden directly in front of your house. Its richly colored blooms and fragrant herbs represent the feelings that give your relationship its special flavor and the right spice, as well as those that simply decorate your farmhouse. The combination of use and beauty appeals to both of you as a couple, but also is enjoyed by others who live with you or visit you: your parents, siblings, children, stepchildren, grandchildren, friends, and strangers. Such a garden is a sensual counterweight to the distant fields that you work with plow and tractor, as flowers and herbs require love and tender care. You need experience to know what can be planted together and what should be kept separate. You need taste so that the colors go well together. But all of the time that you put into this garden of emotions comes back around to you.

In this garden, in a hidden corner, stands your love tent. Surrounded by your lovingly tended plants and in the protection of the homestead, it is almost more beautiful here than before when it stood all alone and was the center of your universe.

- *The right fertilizer:* Don't trample around on the tender blossoms of your partner's emotions. Don't hurt your partner's feelings. Always treat each other with respect. Be careful that you don't contaminate this sensitive field with poisonous comments. Sow friendly words, which work like benevolent healing herbs. Part of the garden is paying attention to the other's dignity. The equality of man and woman forbids emotional blackmail. Never use your feelings or sex to pressure your partner. Don't threaten your partner, and don't put him or her down in front of others.

- *The fruits:* Your homestead doesn't only produce useful things, but also things that are simply fun and bring you joy. Thus your emotional garden provides the right spice in your life and strengthens your feeling of togetherness. You give each other physical closeness, emotional warmth, and sexual intimacy. You take an interest in each other. Without the garden, your homestead would look much bleaker.

Field 3: The Orchard, or the Intellectual Section. Intellectual thought and conversation are often symbolized by an orchard. Here stand all of your "trees of knowledge." You tend them through meaningful conversations together. Don't just talk about who does what, but rather also about your ideas about technology, art, sports, nature, or politics. Together, you consider global and social structures and changes. With the orchard you cultivate the cultural landscape. Here you find the right to form your own opinion. Enjoy being a free citizen and not a

 servant. Grant each other this freedom of thought. Have passionate discussions, but don't censor your partner and don't tell your partner what he or she should think. Then you will harvest the delicious fruits of knowledge as a couple, which you would not have been able to reach on your own.

- *The right fertilizer:* Have conversations about your own interests and what moves your partner. Learn from each other. Talk every day about yourselves as a couple, not just when you argue or when you need to talk through something. Find friends or groups who aren't only fun to hang out with, but also interested in intellectual exchange. Let your partner take part in your intellectual development. Support each other by staying curious, always being happy to learn something new, and further developing your awareness.

- *The fruits:* You can understand and express yourself better. You become more mature and get to know your partner's uniqueness. You don't only have a common project with your partner, but also a common world of ideas, which was overlooked in the classic two-field system. In this field, shared ideas grow visions and symbols, which allow you to develop into a strong, intellectually connected couple so you can also make it through a bad crop in the material wheat field.

Field 4: The Potato Field, or the Soul Section. Like many other plants, potatoes grow underground. Their leaves above ground betray nothing of the valuable life energy that they store underground. In the same way, the fruits of your soul grow in the depths and like potatoes, they must be patiently dug out. Take your time. Talk about what's going on in your soul. Tell each other your dreams. Agree to listen to each other when you need to whine and just share your difficulties with another person. Understand that it's not a reproach when your partner opens his or her heart and complains about you. The emotional potato field doesn't look attractive. The work you do here can be hard, dusty, and sometimes muddy. But it's worth it because it is the staple food of your relationship.

- *The right fertilizer:* Respect the inner values of your partner. Learn the art of seeing your partner's beautiful soul and not only his or her physical beauty (which, in contrast to the beauty of the soul, usually suffers over the course of the years). Reveal yourself to each other; empathize with one another. Be happy to see how your partner grows older and more mature.
- *The fruits:* Potatoes are especially nourishing and durable. Good fruits of the soul have the same quality. They nourish and hold out for a long time. When you get a sense of your partner's innermost depths, understand your partner, and handle him or her with care, you don't have to worry about the survival of your relationship. Even when it doesn't go so well with your finances and time budget (the wheat field), with the emotions (the flower garden), or with your views (the orchard), as long as you have your soulful reserves in your potato cellar, you'll get everything else under control again.

Field 5: The Vineyard, or the Spiritual Section. The classical image of spiritual growth is the vineyard. Wine grapes flourish only in just the right climate and require careful cultivation. Getting a mature wine out of the grapes requires further processes

between the wine press and the cellar. But if you understand the art of wine-making, you've mastered the crowning achievement of agriculture. A homestead with a vineyard—that is something noble. When you as a couple also cultivate the field of spirituality, you can enjoy the full richness of a relationship.

- *The right fertilizer:* To create a spiritual climate, start with careful conversations about your own beliefs. A regular exchange of ideas assists your shared spiritual journey. Accompany your partner in his or her own inner growth by including your partner quietly in your meditations or prayers. Have yourselves be blessed together; bless each other. Collect healing, strengthening spiritual images and symbols. Devote one area of your living space to this. This way, you will become intimate spiritual partners. You help each other reach new heights of reality. You come into contact with a higher source, which gives you confirmation, meaning, and connection.

- *The fruits:* Spiritual intimacy is a special fruit perceived by couples to be an extraordinary gift, like a special vintage of wine. They dive together into the great existence of life, which envelops and supports them.

Cultivate Missing or Poorly Tended Fields of Your Relationship. What do you do when a field is missing? As long as neither of you notice the lack, it won't immediately bring your relationship off-kilter. Starting with Field 1, try to gradually reclaim the other fields of your homestead. It's never too late, as long as both of you are willing.

Sometimes one of you will say, "Something is missing in our relationship," and feel that one of your fields is no longer sufficient. This person is the first to feel hungry and will look for a new field that you can farm together. This results in a typical difficulty in the homestead phase: you and your partner have to adjust to your different styles, scope, and pace of personal development.

If you want to unlock something new for your life, your inner motivation is important: are you doing something "for yourself" or "for yourself as someone who is part of a couple?" Don't give up too quickly if your partner doesn't get into it right away. Keep trying to cultivate that new field. Do it in such a way that your partner sees what's happening, so that you both are always keeping your relationship in focus.

Your Kitchen and Pantry: Nourish Your Relationship

For a happy and content life together, you need the fruits of all five fields. Money and possessions alone (Field 1) can't satisfy you. Neither

can emotions alone (Field 2). If you're intellectually starving (Field 3), you can't be contented with money, sex, or expensive vacations. Every person hungers for philosophical exchange or spiritual resonance. The menu for couples should thus contain a diverse, stimulating fare. You can't always rely on a harvest from all five fields at the same time, so you need reserves to nourish and provide for you when one field has a small yield. You could call this the economy of the heart.

Marriage and family psychologist John Gottman studied couples for thirty years. Couples volunteered to spend a weekend in his marriage laboratory, an apartment near Seattle outfitted with cameras, where they allowed their everyday interactions to be observed (only bed and bath were off-limits to the cameras). These observations, in combination with interviews, showed not only what causes marriages to fail, but above all what keeps happy marriages going. The results, translated into the imagery of the homestead: happy couples nibble daily on little relationship "snacks." Doing so allows them to build up reserves for difficult times, which strike even the happiest relationships.

The Basic Principle of Stockpiling: The 5-to-1 Rule. Negative experiences with your partner are ravenous energy robbers. They eat away at the relationship. Positive experiences, on the other hand, are fertile energizers. You need quite a lot of them, though, to balance out a negative experience. Gottman's insight was that in a relationship, the ratio of positive to negative comments and interactions should be 5 to 1. One argument or negative comment is balanced out by five supporting, loving messages or actions. This is a lot! You should always stock up on these positive qualities and interactions. Competent couples have happy relationships because they are always refilling their pantry through constructive behavior patterns. If it's filled to the brim with positive relationship experiences, they can make it through difficult times more easily.

In addition to the 5-to-1 rule, Gottman created an extremely useful list of good couple behavior. We call them the seven basic recipes, from which you can prepare all the good things your relationship needs, using the reserves of your five relationship fields.

First Recipe: Update Your Partner-Wiki. As a member of a couple, you carry inside of you a never-complete encyclopedia article about your partner. Like an entry in the interactive Internet encyclopedia Wikipedia, it contains all of your knowledge of your partner's unique traits and particularities: how he likes his eggs cooked, that he likes jazz, her favorite perfume, what kinds of films she loves, and so on. For a strong relationship, it's important that these facts be as current and accurate as possible.

- *Get rid of outdated information.* On Wikipedia, anyone who discovers an error in an article can edit it; so all authors contribute to an improved version. As a couple, you should do the same because your partner will change: maybe he switched to scrambled eggs, but still loves jazz; her taste in perfume is totally different now, but she still watches romantic comedies. If you sit down and ask each other, you'll be amazed how much has changed in your partner!

- *Stay curious.* Think of yourself as a researcher who is trying to find out as much as possible about the other person's tower. In the tower you come across all kinds of half-hidden, musty objects: old family myths, unconscious wishes, fears, and unresolved spiritual questions. Allow yourself and your partner to continuously make new exploratory trips into both towers, because these long-familiar places also undergo transformations. Habits and preferences change just like the opinions that you've heard from your partner. Don't assume— ask! Be glad when you continually discover new sides of your life partner. The more you get to know your partner's tower, the better you know him or her. If you remain curious and attentive to your partner every day, this web stays elastic to better protect your relationship in times of change.

Second Recipe: Admire and Touch Each Other. The most elementary ingredients of a fulfilling relationship are your positive feelings for each other. Affection and admiration keep the kitchen fires going and give you as a couple a comforting warmth in your home. Gottman's research shows that 94 percent of couples who view their marriage as positive feel a high level of warmth for each other and are optimistic about their ability to hold on to this warmth in the future.

- *Thank goodness I have you!* Showing mutual appreciation strengthens a couple enormously. Compliment your partner. Say what makes you happy about being together. Speak with pride and respect about your partner. Don't ever put down your partner in front of others. If you agree with the other's ideas, suggestions, or solutions, praise him or her explicitly. Mark positive experiences together: "It was fantastic that we were able to do that together." Save the best place in your pantry for these good experiences. Collect symbols that remind you of them. This treasure trove will help you get through difficult times.
- *Maintain physical contact.* Touch the other person as often as you can. Hold hands occasionally as you're walking, kiss each other when saying hello and good-bye, and cuddle up  together in front of the TV. Use all of these little forms of physical affection to bring warmth into your relationship. Everything that makes both of you feel good is good. Sex is naturally a part of this, but the erotic heights you reach together can't replace that little "cuddle bank."

Third Recipe: Turn to Each Other. Positive attention is made up of countless small experiences of closeness. Good couples are always thinking about We, and they find their way to each other in a thousand small, everyday matters: "I had the strangest dream last night," or "Guess what happened to my sister yesterday!" All of these are good openers for paying attention to each other.

- *Turn on your receiver.* Think of the super flirt rule (see Simplifying Idea 7: Learn to Flirt—the Art of Building Your Tent, in Ch. 2) and don't just be interesting, be interested. Confirm with a nod or a yes that you've listened and understood. Ask for clarification. Be interested in feelings. Ask how the other person's day was. Even if you can't do anything about his or her bad mood or irritation at the moment—just hearing you say, "Thanks for telling me about it," does your partner good. Solidarity is especially nourishing: "If something is bothering you, it's our problem, not just yours. We'll get through it together." When you have hurt or angered your partner, admit it: "I can see that I've hurt you. I'm sorry."

- *Leave a sign.* Show that you're thinking about the other person. When you go shopping, bring your partner something that will make him or her smile. Call during the day when you know that your partner had an important meeting in the morning, and ask how it went. If you can't always have breakfast together, leave a note on the table: "I'll be thinking about you today." Be imaginative, but don't overdo it. Allow the other person his or her own ways of expressing him- or herself.

- *Understanding comes before advice.* When your partner has a problem, you don't have to solve it for him or her, but you should offer your full attention. Empathize first before giving advice. Let the other person tell you everything, and listen calmly, sympathize, and comfort him or her. Take his or her side. Don't judge the situation, whether rationally or morally. Show your solidarity—"It's us against them," and express your affection with a loving gesture. Then you may offer to help find a solution.

Fourth Recipe: Let Yourself Be Influenced. In a relationship, there are often different perspectives sitting side by side. Gottman's studies suggest that men find it especially difficult to share power and allow themselves to be influenced by their partner's opinion. Again, it's a question of a fair division of power: How should money be spent? Who does the housework? Who decides whose career is more important, how the children are raised, where to go on vacation? Gottman also found that most problems disappear when the man is ready to find the reasonable demands contained in his partner's complaints.

- *Accept each other.* Even when you have opposing ideas, open your heart to the other's position. Signal with a yes that you remain open to listening and engaging with the other's thoughts. Don't enter into the communication "strike" of silence, turning a deaf ear or running away. Register the feelings of the other person without comment. Summarize what the other person said: "If I understand it right, you want/ you think . . ."
- *Be diplomatic.* Two people represent two realities. Part of the secret of a happy relationship is allowing a common project to emerge from differing viewpoints. Transform your own demands into requests. Consider it a personal success when you can give in and show yourself ready to compromise. But don't keep a tally to use against the other.

Fifth Recipe: Solve Your Solvable Problems. Gottman analyzed how good couples deal with conflicts. He found that they have a firm argument schema in five steps, with which they can surmount conflicts without damaging their relationship. He called this the "Good

Manners Schema." In this system, you grant your partner the respect that you would show a guest or a friend. These steps are as follows:

- *Take the gentle approach.* In 80 percent of all marriages, women bring up touchy subjects, while men attempt to avoid the discussion. Often, the man isn't even aware of the problem, while the woman assumes that he must have noticed something by now. For this reason, women should begin such a conversation with a friendly tone, without being rude or deprecating. Gottman's research revealed that discussions always end the way they began!
- *Start the rescue attempt.* When it comes to conflicts, it's important to know when to step on the brakes so that things don't escalate. Formulate your reproaches "elastically"; see that your position is relative. Always allow for the fact that your partner could be right.
- *Compromise.* Put the white flag up every now and then, and show your willingness to negotiate. Accept the little rescue attempts that your partner makes: an agreeing nod, a smile, or an admission of your own.
- *Tolerate the other's mistakes.* Let go of the "if only my partner were different" attitude. When dealing with conflicts, it's not about changing the other person, but about finding a way to live with each other. When you get angry about something about your partner (he never does the dishes), recall a positive quality about your partner (he has our finances in order). When your partner has botched something up, offer him or her the chance to make up for it. Be realistic—you would have differences with another partner, too.

Sixth Recipe: Overcome Seemingly Irreconcilable Differences. In addition to solvable problems, there will also always be a few seemingly unsolvable stalemates between two people: the one wants children, the other doesn't. One wants to live in the country, the other in the city. Both get bogged down in their own position because each demands that the other give up a stubborn attitude.

> **Simplifying Tip:** The resistance usually comes from the fact that each of you has a certain picture of what's important to you and absolutely must be fulfilled. Usually it's still slumbering, hidden in your subconscious. Search for it with the following sentence: "My dream when it comes to this issue is . . . " Tell yourself about it, whether or not this dream can be realized. Then look for small steps that can bring you closer to your dream without hurting the other person. ■

Seventh Recipe: Create a Shared Purpose. Investigate together the basic principles that touch both your hearts. What are your deepest personal goals? Build your homestead together on the basis of these.

 There is room for the dreams, visions, and goals of both of you under the roof of a happy relationship. The most important secret of happy couples is to build both people's life dreams into the shared relationship and to help each other to realize them.

> **Simplifying Tip:** Take turns telling each other your family stories, and find in them the hidden positive values that you absolutely don't want to live without (generosity, helpfulness, modesty, love of nature, etc.). Ask your partner to make room for these values in your relationship together. Find a family member whom you both like and who you can imagine is genuinely happy about your relationship. Ideally, you'll find someone from your grandparents' generation or a more distant relative. It can even be someone who has passed away. The blessing upon you, which is greater than you, becomes visible through this person. ■

Simplifying Idea 12:
Live Together Intelligently

In modern life, a relationship is serious as soon as you go to IKEA together. If you move in together, in addition to your shared inner space, you literally create external spaces for your relationship; you furnish a new apartment, deciding on furniture, floor coverings, and drapes. You find out who's good with technology and who gets the job of head designer. Much has to be decided: who cooks, who cleans, who is responsible for which rooms?

Living and Housework

The executive secretary of a large firm told us once that planning a children's birthday party is at least as complex a task as organizing a board meeting! Managing a household and a family is not a "lowly" activity. The thousands of little tasks and considerations that you have to take care of at home every day have a deeper meaning for you and your partnership. The follow-ing method will help you cooper-ate on the potentially irritating and argument-inducing task of housework and may even deepen your relationship.

The Simplifying Room Therapy. Which areas of your home need attention? Usually, this involves six activities: cleaning, organizing, repairing, clearing out, rearranging, and decorating. These projects correspond to six levels of your inner person: health, security, clarity, serenity, flexibility, and harmony. If you shape and order your actual spaces according to these six simplifying principles, you undergo a healing process for your home that will do you and your relationship good. When your home is harmonized, it releases the six benevolent energies—for the two of you, your children, and all of your guests.

1. *Health through cleanliness.* Your home is a place of constant cleaning up: You wash and bathe. You wash your laundry in the washing machine. You wash fruits and vegetables before you eat them. You wash dishes; clean off your shoes; sweep, mop and vacuum the floors; dust furniture; clean windows; and so on. Our advice for simplification is cleanliness means protection against annoying odors, infections, and pests. Think of cleaning as a family health precaution that everyone contributes to and everyone has to learn. Create a cleaning schedule that lists all of the necessary tasks. Each housekeeping task is also housekeeping for your soul. Try it with the following idea in mind: when I clean, I wash myself free of negative feelings and thoughts.

2. *Clarity through organization.* This doesn't cost anything but time and endurance, but it does require the right storage spaces (e.g., closets, drawers, shelves, files). You should have 10 to 20 percent of the storage space left over when everything is put away. The question of "who picks up around here, and who doesn't" often makes for unconscious power games. Have the "mess-makers" nothing to say for themselves? Here is some simplifying advice: for your shared spaces, come up with rules that apply to all family members. For the children's rooms, make a few rules that correspond to the ages of the children. Decide together which things belong where ("Everything has its place."), and agree that whoever uses them will return them to their proper place when finished. With orderly habits, everyone gains clarity, structure, and even more free time. Open space and well-organized rooms give your subconscious a sense of security and familiarity. You gain a feeling of your own worth and sovereignty.

3. *Security through repairs.* Furniture and appliances break or get old and have to be refurbished. Apartments and houses require regular maintenance that usually require a specialist. This task must

be delegated and paid for. Here is some advice for simplification: to minimize the financial burden, set aside a small amount of money regularly so you can distribute the total costs equally throughout the year. The expenses will occur multiple times per year. The gain, however, is that when everything works, you avoid danger, and  your home offers comfort and security. Likewise, injuries to your soul also "require repair" and can be healed. There are injuries that you can heal yourself and ones that you should bring to a friend or therapist. This isn't a luxury; rather, it is important for the safety and security of your inner life.

4. *Serenity through clearing out.* In much-used rooms and in small apartments, this is a constant task. It can be hard to give things away when you haven't let go of them inside. Our simplifying advice for this is when you sort out papers, clothing, and things you don't use, give them a "blessing" for their journey as you give them away, donate them, or sell them. Trust that something good will come out of those things. You'll no longer find it painful to give things away, but rather feel a sense of relief. Do this regularly, ideally every month on a set day. Because it helps you detach from the past, you move more freely in the here and now. Your soul learns something from this: he or she who lets go is buoyed up—and is more serene!

5. *Flexibility through rearranging.* By this we mean moving furniture around or repurposing entire rooms. You can make the children's room into a guest room or office. Many shy away from change because they are afraid of the transitional chaos. Here is our advice for simplification: right from the start, imagine the wonderful end

result, and keep that image in mind. Talk about it in detail. The better you both can imagine living in your new spaces, the less confusion there will be. If you manage to constantly reshape your living space, then the same thing can happen with your psyche and your relationship. Nothing enriches your life more than a developing soul.

6. *Harmony through decoration.* Now comes the fun part. Many people fear that decorating is too expensive. Our advice for simplification is figure out whether the room wouldn't actually gain more harmony by the removal of a few things, by your limiting of the color palette, or through softer lighting. Less is often more; simpler is

often nicer. Beauty and harmony are attractive: they draw friends in and increase your feeling of self-worth. You learn to unfold your creative ability and apply it to your surroundings. Your inner life will become more beautiful along with your home.

Four Healing Feelings

If one of the partners is struggling with problems that awaken negative feelings inside, it can burden your relationship. You feel these emotions as unchecked anger, rage, grumpiness, or depression. Such feelings are useful, though, once you learn to understand them as messages from your subconscious—messages that want your attention. Something that feels downright painful can actually be a source of healing. Find out together which feeling is flaring up most strongly. The secret messages of your four feelings are the following:

- *Anger.* Something happened that you didn't want to happen. Formulate concretely what that is. *The healing aspect:* don't expect miracles from your partner. Instead, take care of changes or corrections yourself.

- *Sadness*. You've lost something or are missing something that you need or want. *The healing aspect:* learn to accept the loss in small steps.
- *Worry*. You would like to change something, but it's not within your power. *The healing aspect:* let go of the problem. Learn to forget it or to leave it to greater hands than yours.
- *Fear*. You've been warned of a failure, a loss, or an injury. *The healing aspect:* accept help. Overcome your shame, and talk out your fear. Don't hesitate to ask for support and assistance.

The Double-Strategy Defense. Use these healing and recovery strategies *together*. Grant each other twenty minutes alone, and write out what is bothering you. Only then can you stop repressing a negative feeling. Attribute that feeling to your own experience, and don't ever chalk it up to your partner.

Arrange for twenty minutes of mutual attention, and tell each other what is bothering you at the moment. When you express the whole truth about your feelings, you will often already see the healing solutions flickering behind them. The negative feeling disappears as soon as you gain understanding for each other. And your love finally has free rein again.

The Five Most Important Words

"There's nothing you can do." This is the phrase that can revolutionize your relationship. Five magical words with which a husband can calm his wife and a wife her husband. Women like to air their feelings. This often comes across to her partner as a reproach or accusation, even if she doesn't mean it that way. Therefore, John Gray suggests that women pause a minute and make listening easier for their husbands by saying, "I'm glad that you're listening to me. Even if it sometimes seems like I'm blaming you, really I don't mean to. There's nothing you can do."

The Countdown of Love

These are the most beautiful words that can combat a loveless relationship:

- The six most beautiful words: "I admit that I was wrong."
- The five most beautiful words: "You did a wonderful job."
- The four most beautiful words: "What do you think?"
- The three most beautiful words: "Can I help?"
- The two most beautiful words: "Thank you."
- The most beautiful word: "We."

And the most beautiful of all: understanding without words!

Simplifying Idea 13: Clarify the Children Question

In problem-oriented societies, children are often reduced to the difficulties they bring with them: noise, mess, time, and the money that they cost. In short, children are viewed from the "complicated" perspective. We would like to encourage you to regard children with "simplifying eyes." We're certain that the largest happiness you can experience on your homestead is the arrival of new occupants who have you—and you alone—to thank for their existence. Children make your homestead into a vital, lively, and especially lovable place!

An Irrevocable Relationship

The more noncommittal relationships become, the less couples remain faithful to each other for their whole lives. Temporary relationships develop, suited to a certain phase in your life. With a child it's different: a child can't occupy just a particular phase of your life. Having a child means entering into a lifelong relationship. Family sociologist Bernhard Nauck hits the nail on the head: "Parenthood is the only obligation left in the modern multi-option society that can't be renounced."

Over and over we hear discussions in politics and the media about the costs of a child. Couples ask themselves: can we afford a(nother) child? Women ask themselves: how do I juggle career and children? Men ask themselves: can't we be happier as just the two of us?

You can collect and debate arguments for and against children your whole life long. But this question can't be answered with reason alone. So we offer you the following advice for simplification:

Open Yourself up to Your Future Parent-Power

We are convinced that you carry a personal navigation system within you to guide your way in the land of love. Each person has a vision of how his life should look, but only a few people have access to this picture. They mistrust their life-GPS and put their faith instead in external "facts" that they read in newspapers. They trust what their parents, teachers, or friends say. They don't dare to ask anymore what answer is slumbering inside of them, what assignment they may have received from life, what dream they should transform into reality. It is a tragedy how much bravery is no longer thought and how much greatness is no longer done.

Place both of your life-navigation systems next to each other when you move into the homestead. Picture it: How do I want to live? How do I want to live together with you? How do we want to live? What ideas flash up inside of you? If both of you find a clear inner picture of having your own children, then you will probably have these children and love them and find some way to feed them, regardless of any material or occupational obstacles!

But your inner picture isn't quite so simple. You also find inside you a colorful jumble of experiences, television reports, and collective opinion. With the following visualization exercises, you can clarify your inner picture.

Vision 1: Observing Babies. Pay attention to pregnant women and babies around you. Touch the baby things in the children's section of the department store. Go down the toy aisles. Watch kids on the playground. Do you feel longing, envy, or sadness when you see another man or woman with a baby in the arms? Are you touched?

■ *Pull yourself away from your biological clock by making a clear decision.* For women, the window of time for having children is considerably smaller than for men. Regardless of your age, when you know that you want to have children or if you suddenly feel the urge to have a baby, then the child question should be on the table. Your partner must take the time to ask himself this question, too. Postponing it keeps you both tied to the "principle of not deciding," which at first may seem like a privilege: "We're still young; we have time." As time goes on, though, you both come under precisely the pressure that you wanted to avoid.

■ *Assess the actual value of your career.* Often, a couple chooses not to have a child because of their careers. But have you really both honestly weighed the two against each other? Stephan Covey's famous question is a worthwhile thought experiment: can you imagine laying on your deathbed and saying to yourself, "If only I had spent more time in the office during my life!"? Covey also recommends writing your own obituary, in two versions: one for the wildest-dreams course of your career, and one for the worst imaginable. In reality, you will probably end up somewhere in between. Does this fulfill you? Does it make up for the lack of children? Consciously transfer your perception of your own worth from your career to your private life. Which personal qualities can you count on here? Have you fully developed them?

■ *Unlock your true potential.* Every child taps into a never-before-imagined energy reserve in his or her parents. When your partner wants to have a child with you, he or she perceives this potential intuitively. Your partner trusts that you will develop this potential together through parenthood. If you both trust each other, you become visionaries for each other and develop your inner potential to the greatest possible degree.

Vision 2: Your Inner Grandparent. With your eyes closed, imagine your ideal grandfather or grand-mother. This should have nothing to do with your actual grandparents. See in your mind's eye this person approaching you. What does he or she do? How does it make you feel?

When we do this little exercise in our semi-nars, the same thing always happens: almost all the participants start smiling. The mood in the room is filled with love, goodness, and joy. Some even come to tears. They describe the inner wisdom, generosity, and seren-ity that radiates from this person. They have the feeling that they've been longing for this figure forever. They feel happiest when this per-son embraces them, and they don't want this person to ever go away. Not one of these imagined beings was egocentric or materialistic. None of them had fear or financial worry. None was concerned with ques-tions of status or demanded their personal independence. All of the fantasy grandparents were devoted, free, and spiritually rich.

When we tell our seminar participants who their ideal grandparent really is, they are profoundly amazed. The grandmother or grandfather that is waiting within you to come into the light of reality is you your-self. When doing this exercise, your soul shows itself for a minute in its ripest form. It is your own future self that you see and embrace there. This moment is so heartfelt because you are in agreement with your highest potential. It gives you an idea of your goal, which you could reach in twenty, thirty, or forty years—if you find a way to let your soul transform into this wonderful being.

- *Try skipping over your obstacles.* For some people, this imaginary detour as a grandparent helps them approach the question of their own children. Anyone who wants to become such a wonderful grandfather or benevolent grandmother naturally has to have his or her own children first. By calling up your inner grandparent, you ally yourself with your future rich and free self. It is stronger than you are today. It will awaken your potential and the strength that you need for your life with children.

- *Forget the myth of the right moment.* Don't wait forever. Don't postpone it indefinitely. Stop believing that there will someday be an objectively perfect time for a child. It simply doesn't exist! Every wish for a child, as experienced therapists know, is accompanied with ambivalent feelings. "Can we manage it at all?" couples wonder, even the ones who had a child "at the right time." Reality can change from one moment to the next, and you could suddenly find yourself in completely different circumstances. On the other hand, a path appears under your feet when you start to walk it. This goes for twenty-year-olds as well as forty-year-olds. Even the best planning doesn't take  the place of fundamental trust in the future. Find role models who are personally encouraging for you in your circle of friends, hook up with a good social and family-friendly network in your immediate surroundings, and motivate each other to be brave and resolved.

- *Trust the wisdom of your soul.* There is, however, a right moment for a child that the soul perceives, and which does not necessarily correspond to your external economic circumstances.

Vision 3: Visualize Your Future Child.
First, ask yourself: How would our child look? Where is it right now? Imagine that the child asks each of you individually: "May I come?" How do you and your partner answer this question? Talk this over with love. When
you both have the feeling that the other is looking
you lovingly in the eye and saying, "Yes, I want to have a(nother) child with you," then there is space in your relationship. If you both agree, then love can flow, and the baby is invited to come. Then *both* parents will handle the external circumstances. That is the most important prerequisite for a child.

Vision 4: Your Family Table. How many children do you have room for in your soul? Close your eyes and think fifteen years into the future. Imagine your dream house. Imagine going into the dining room, and setting the table for a family dinner, with all the details—glasses, dishes, silverware, drinks, food for parents and children. How many plates can you put down? How big is your table? This exercise is particularly surprising for men. When they hear the word *child*, they
usually think of an infant, of changing diapers, and of screaming babies and shut themselves off. But when they think of a big family around a dining room table, of a little family orchestra, or of the big family photo at their own seventieth birthday—then the whole thing looks quite different.

More and more people find their way to
this large table with many children through a new
partner who has children from a previous relationship. Suddenly there are three, four, or even more children at the table of a patchwork family—an image that in practice often turns out to be more pleasant than was feared.

Don't Be Afraid of Your Own Shortcomings

Children open up a natural path to adulthood. Pregnancy, birth, and life with a newborn bring "our shortcomings into the world," as psychotherapist Eva-Maria Zurhorst says. A baby has no disguises. It is pure, genuine being. Children help their parents to devote themselves more and more to love. Each touch, comfort, encouragement, feeding, waking, and calming takes away a little bit of narcissism. Your own desires, your own wishes, your own life goals suddenly have to be measured against the great existential experiences of pure existence, embodied in a child. The child doesn't only reveal your shortcomings; it also awakens the gigantic potential to love that slumbers in you as parents.

You Don't Have to Be Superparents. In our psychologically aware society, many people doubt that they can really become good parents—perhaps because they didn't have great parents themselves or because they watch Supernanny help clueless parents on TV. For a long time, psychology blamed parents one-sidedly: upbringing was at fault for everything. Now it's thought that the development of a child is only one-third determined by its upbringing; one-third is rooted in its genes, and the other third comes from the social environment and individual personality. Besides this, the current generation of parents are also starting out with much more pedagogical knowledge than any other generation. So your chances of being good parents are better than ever before.

Relationships Without Children

For a few generations now, effective methods of contraception have allowed sex to be separated from procreation. Children and relationships are no longer automatically associated with one another. "We can be happy without children," is a phrase many couples say today. Other couples would like to have children, but despite all of their effort they are unable to. Here we have a few simplifying suggestions for how to have a fulfilling and happy relationship without children.

Avoid a One-Sided Decision. It's not uncommon for women or men who want to have children to spend their best child-bearing years with a partner who "isn't ready to settle down and start a family," or even hides the fact that he or she doesn't want children at all. Asking your partner to stay in a relationship without children for your sake is a huge sacrifice, one that should be returned in kind with a similarly heroic gift of love. Otherwise, your partner will eventually come to be very resentful, and this could destroy the relationship. So it's best to be honest and not give false hope. Then he or she can find a partner who wants to have children. Women  and men who leave a relationship for this reason are often refreshingly direct with their next partners: "I want you—but also as the father (or mother) of our children."

Don't Speak Badly About Couples with Children. Sometimes it can seem like a relief for childless couples to list the disadvantages of children or to bad-mouth bad parenting. But when you put others down, your soul and your spirit become small and narrow. On the other hand, people who do have children should not disparage childless couples as "self-centered," "career-obsessed," or "freeloaders." Just like in the "war between the sexes," the one who attacks others is above all waging war against him- or herself.

A Childless Couple Can Find a "Spiritual Child." If you both definitely want to live without children, then you can't pass on to your own children what you received from your parents. So to keep the great stream of giving flowing, you should instead find a "spiritual child" who is close to both of your hearts. Beyond work and free time, do something for the good of humanity.

Consider Childlessness an Opportunity. If you want children but can't have them, this can be a difficult situation for both of you. Talk about your pain with each other, share your struggles, and don't let your partner go through it alone. We know that it helps to find a farewell ritual through which you can peacefully and clearly end this phase of your lives that is full of disappointed hopes. Accepting that you must go without children can bind you more deeply together as a couple.

Simplifying Idea 14: Make Your Life Together Easier

During the long phase in the homestead you accomplish the essential work of your life. Here you create what lasts. But this involves work and effort, and every now and then the long road will feel too long for you. We've compiled here the typical complaints and with them, tips for better, happier ways to deal with these complaints—ways that are time-tested and ready to use. Simplifying your love means there's always a way. It's always worthwhile to struggle on. No one

has to sacrifice themselves, no one has to give up. At the end of every struggle you will look back and be able to say, "Yep, it was hard. But it was worth it!"

Escape the Nagging Trap

The classic complaints from mothers are, "I feel left all alone with the children. Everything depends on me. My partner isn't around enough. He never asks how we're all doing—it doesn't interest him at all." The classical complaints of fathers: "I give it my all every day for her and the children, bring home the bacon for everyone, but that doesn't count. She just nags me. I never have time to do anything fun." More and more, the solution to the dilemma seems to be, "We'll separate and then we'll both be free." The serious disadvantage to this is that life is even more complicated by divorce. There have to be other solutions. Here are some:

Translate the Accusation. The woman's sigh, "You're away from home too much," corresponds to her inner feeling, "I'm too tied to this home." A study at Harvard University showed that feelings of overwork and discontent are especially severe for women who have no or little activity outside of the household. Working mothers with household duties are just as exhausted, but don't blame their partners for it as much. Women who work primarily from home are just as discontented as full-time housewives, because the home becomes a demanding space that she is more at the mercy of than the man and which she never escapes—women still do 80 percent of the housework, even when both partners work full time!

Women Must Defend Their Equality. When the children are still small, many women feel especially "tied up," "locked in," and robbed of their personal freedom. Being a mother is a round-the-clock job. The woman is also less financially independent at this time, because she is at least partly going without her own income. At the same time, she sees that parenting doesn't have this same effect for the man. Despite his burdens, her working husband has it both ways: children and flexibility, which she painfully misses. When they have children, most women lose some of their equality (e.g., control over their time and money, mobility). So she complains to him and demands compensation: he has to help out more in the family. He defends himself against the bad mood at home, which takes away the last bit of his refuge: he's not allowed to relax at home or anywhere else. And he always has to feel guilty because he "gets" to go to work.

Recognize the Warning Signs. When it starts boiling inside of you like a volcano ready to erupt, and you start to feel resentful of your partner, it's a sign that you're not taking care of yourself. Constantly sacrificing yourself is the worst thing you can do, according to therapists (and husband and wife) Patty Howell and Ralph Jones. Resentment is your soul's way of telling you that your batteries are empty. No matter how much you take your silent anger or loud rage out on your partner, your children, or your whole surroundings, resentment will stay as long as you don't establish balance between caring for your children and caring for yourself.

Give Yourself Some Freedom. Swiss relationship therapist Rosemarie Welter-Enderlin has formulated an important equalizer for a fair partnership: both parent partners must be able to continue to operate as adult individuals. Use the following two-part question to check how much freedom each of you really has:

Question 1: Can the woman leave the family now and then to retreat to her private sphere without first having to arrange child care and meals? Does she have ready access to time and money when she does?

Question 2: Can the man do the things he likes to do now and then without it involving either work responsibilities or negligence toward his family?

Negotiate a Fair Arrangement. Using these questions, talk over your needs. Work out a reasonable treaty that gives each of you enough individual "adult freedom" every month. Talk openly, but be tough. For example: one day during the week he must be home at five so she can have a free night, and one evening a week he doesn't have to come home right away, but can do things with friends or go play sports as long as he wants. At least four days per month are just hers alone; on two weekends he takes care of the children and takes responsibility for the household (including grocery shopping, cooking, and cleaning), on the other two she does. Divorced fathers often find that the obligatory

weekends with their children mean that they actually spend more time with them than they did while married!

Be Absolutely Reliable. This schedule must be rigidly followed and heroically defended against threats from the office—it is an opportunity for the man to demonstrate his manliness to his boss or customers! Respect this schedule unconditionally: reliability is a cornerstone of love. The more reliable you prove to be to each other, the more your love will grow despite the burdens of everyday life. Once a year, stop and check whether the agreement still makes sense or whether it's time to renegotiate.

Divide up Obligations. First there's career, education, raising children, and managing a household; then tack on elderly parents, a dog, or a garden to take care of, plus problems that arise at kindergarten or school and you can easily reach your limit. Health problems and arguments are the consequences. Here the only help is an objective analysis with everyone involved, where obligations can be reduced, delegated, or removed altogether: the smaller the children, the simpler you should make it. The older the children get, the more obligations can be taken on and divided up fairly.

Build a Network. Get connected to other families who have children around the same ages and who live nearby: form carpools with other mothers to bring children to soccer practice or music lessons, and take each other's children for a  weekend now and then. Involve the fathers, too: who can do what especially well and contribute? Call the other families about a special sale you notice at the store to see if they want one, too. Put together a "contingency plan" with these partner families in case one of the mothers gets sick. In the long term, this kind of network stabilizes your relationship, because everything doesn't have to depend on the partner.

Patchwork Families: Stepparents and Stepchildren

A divorce is always terrible, for both partners and especially for the children. If you have children and have found a new partner or if your new partner has children, it can all seem very complicated at first. There are a lot of opportunities for everyone involved to behave poorly and hurt someone's feelings. But it can also make your life more colorful and surprising, just like a patchwork quilt. Here are the most important simplifying suggestions.

Don't Ask Too Much of Your Children. More than anything, a child wishes for his or her parents to love and appreciate one another. It causes inner conflict for the child when he or she has to choose  between the two of them. Often parents want to give their children the choice of whom they want to live with after a separation. Our simplifying advice is don't do it. On this point, the parents must agree. Don't put your child in the terrible position of having to choose between the two of you and thereby disappoint the other one. A child has a right to both parents. Forcing a child to choose between his or her father and mother (which can also happen in problematic marriages) results in an unsure, indecisive adult.

Don't Talk Badly About Each Other in Front of Your Child. This is one of the most common errors of single or remarried parents: they speak—often with good reason and without bad intentions—badly of the other parent. But the child is made up of 50 percent mother and 50 percent father. If the mother says bad things about the father, the child unconsciously concludes that 50 percent of him- or herself is no good, leading to low self-esteem. Or the child allies her- or himself secretly with the maligned partner and is then angry at the other parent.

> **Simplifying Tip:** The best thing is to not only speak well of your ex, but also to think well of your ex. Say to yourself and to the

child: "He (or she) is a wonderful person, but we simply didn't fit together." ■

Wait, What Was Sex Again?

"My partner isn't interested in sex any-more." "I always have to make the first move, but it didn't used to be that way." "Why are our sex drives so different?" "How can we get a little excitement and romance back into our relationship?" These are the sighs that come up again and again in marriages and relation-ships, sometimes from him, sometimes from her. The following answers for this extremely touchy subject are inspired by the ideas of psychologist Phil McGraw.

Sex Is the Tip of the Iceberg. On the surface, it's all just about your sex life: he or she isn't getting enough or is getting the wrong kind. In most cases, though, this is a cover for the desire for more intimacy, respect, recognition, tenderness, or sensitivity.

For it to work, two people have to change: you and the other person. Some advice for simplification is to start with yourself. How are you contributing to the problem? Only when you can be honest about this may you go to your partner and ask something of him or her.

Sex Is a Pattern. At the beginning of your relationship, there were certain rituals, places, and times when it took place. Now there are a thousand other habits added to your lives from your work, the children, living together, your parents, and so on. It's hard to make room in between all of these things for the happy patterns of the old days. The biggest break comes after the birth of a child: lovers turn into mother and father. They iden-tify with their own parents, who in

their eyes didn't have sex. Some simplifying advice is don't think of being a parent as a new nature, but as a new role, in addition to which you can also play the role of sexual partner and lover.

Visual Excitements. It happens to everyone: you don't look as sexy as you did then. The same goes for your partner. But start again with yourself. Here is a tip for simplification: your self-image is more important than losing weight, a new haircut, or seductive clothing. Say to yourself, "I am not only Mom (or Dad). I'm still a sexy thing." Then act that way. There's always a bit of nostalgia in this: what did your partner always used to like? Nine times out of ten it still works today.

Talk to Each Other. Don't count on your partner reading your mind. You have to put it into words. But how? Our tip for simplification is approach it the way the porcupine approaches sex—very

carefully. Don't make accusations, and don't bring it up during an argument or when you're in the car. Find a good lead-in, ideally a happy memory from earlier times: a photo of the two of you as a young couple, an old movie you always liked.

An important element of sexuality is fantasy. Explore your and your partner's erotic dreams. Listen to everything, and soak it all in. Some advice for simplification is it's not about making all of these dreams a reality. But you can't have erotic closeness when one partner disdains the other's dreams or finds them disgusting or immature. This is just as bad as having too many secrets.

If your fantasies are so strange that you don't dare to say them out loud, write your requests in a love letter. You're not practicing selfish eroticism here, but rather taking your partner with you into your fantasies. He has to feel secure that even in your more daring wishes, he remains the unsurpassable goal of your erotic and romantic energy.

Share the Burden. Get your partner to the point where he or she can say, "Rekindling our sex life is our shared project." Our simplifying advice is to forget the fairy tale of spontaneous sex. In your situation, sex requires preparation; the kids have to go to bed early enough, you have to be awake enough, you have to not watch TV until you're sleepy, and you have to meet each other halfway in your desires.

Open Your Heart. Imagine sex as a garden next to your homestead, which grows and is always changing. Sex is much more than just the act of intercourse. Over the course of the years, you will come to know that light touches, hugs, or closeness are also erotic gifts. Sex is a complete work of art that changes with your body's changes. A woman's body changes after she has children, and many things feel different than they did before. Older men aren't as virile as they once were, and no one expects them to be. Relax, and instead of plastic surgery and Viagra, take the great simplifying medicine of serenity—you don't need a prescription, and there are no risks or side effects.

Thoughts of Escape: When It Gets Uncomfortable at the Homestead

The secret goal of your relationship is to develop a shared spiritual space in which each of you has enough room for what is most precious to him or her. For this space, the oft-mentioned researcher of the unconscious C. G. Jung uses the image of rooms, which fits perfectly with the homestead: each of you has different space requirements for your emotional needs. One of you, whom Jung calls the *Simple One*, only occupies a few small rooms. The other, the *Complicated One*, takes up many rooms and a lot of space. This causes a double dilemma: to the Complicated One, the Simple One has such little space that there isn't enough room. For the Simple One, on the other hand, the Complicated One offers so much space that the Simple One doesn't really know where he or she actually belongs.

Am I Contained in You? Do you have space for me? Is there room in your soul for my soul? These are the crucial questions that can destroy a relationship. This is often what causes someone to have an affair or to pull away emotionally. So it's worth it to address this topic before something happens.

- *If you're the Simple One.* Then you are content with your partner and feel well cared for in the relationship. You are contained in the other person, and the rooms you use in the homestead are enough for you. You appreciate the preferences of your partner and are proud of him or her. Perhaps, though, you also sense that you don't completely satisfy your partner's expectations. You have, as Jung called it, an "unsettling dependency" on your partner, who is a stronger personality or enjoys a higher social standing. You often allow your partner to lead or take priority.

- *If you're the Complicated One.* Then you will always suffer from not being able to find all of yourself within your relationship. You look for new qualities in a partner that can complement your own. You push for expansion in the homestead: plow more fields or add new rooms. For you, your partner is too unrefined, too unsophisticated, or too inarticulate. At the same time, you know how your partner could further develop him- or herself, and you long to experience your partner in a new, equal way.

How Both End up in the Dark Forest. The Simple One realizes that he or she is not enough for the Complicated One and needs to change. This is a shock. The Simple One loses the feeling of security and faces a dilemma: either the Simple One stays how he or she is—which forces the Complicated One back into the confines of the little rooms, feeling like a bird with clipped wings—or the Simple One tries to open him- or herself up to new fields. This isn't easy, because the Simple One does it under the critical eye of the partner and doesn't know if he or she can ever live up to the other's high demands. Or the Simple One reacts with guilty feelings and gives up hope for a fulfilling relationship.

In both cases the Simple One is made to feel insecure. The Simple One loses touch with him- or herself and with the partner. The home-  stead doesn't feel like a familiar home anymore, but becomes gradually uncomfortable—the dark forest casts its shadow all the way here.

The Complicated One wavers between being true to self and being true to the partner. If the Complicated One puts pressure on the other to expand his or her spaces, it makes life in the homestead uncomfortable and later perhaps even unbearable. The Complicated One can try to shape the Simple One in his or her own image and to pull the Simple One "up"—as in the musical *My Fair Lady*, where the language teacher turns a common street girl into an educated lady. But the Complicated One won't get an equal partner this way, just a different one. Another possibility: the Complicated One can retreat to one of his or her many rooms. But it doesn't get lonelier than that.

Whatever the Complicated One does, he or she ends up feeling torn. In the end, the Complicated One looks outside of the relationship for what the Simple One has found inside of it—and the Complicated One finds him- or herself again in the dark forest.

Simple and Complicated Crosswise. In practice, it's rare for one partner to just be complicated and the other just simple. Depending on what aspect of life you're talking about, sometimes one person is contained in the other, sometimes the other way around. In the traditional marriage, it was usually the woman who intellectually had her place within her husband. She let him think and decide for the both of them. The man, on the other hand, was often emotionally contained within his wife. He let her sense and feel for the both of them. And the exact opposite existed as well.

In modern relationships, it's even more complex: here you often find both of you in the position of the Complicated One; the content- ment of the Simple One hardly exists anymore. Both of you accuse the other of having shortcomings and demand that the other change. This leads the couple into a narcissistic dead end: "The other has to change him- or herself into what I want."

How You Can Solve the Dilemma

- *What the Complicated One can do.* Be loyal and patient. Stay in the relationship. C. G. Jung knew from his long psychotherapeutic practice that a separation from an "unsatisfying" partner doesn't really solve this problem. His advice is to endure this dilemma consciously, and call your soul to the rescue. Because the soul always strives for unity, doing so will mobilize your inner strengths. You will find an opportunity to reunite with your inner self, instead of seeking it in another person. The greatest reward for your patience is that you experience yourself as "undivided in yourself." You find more unity in your own depth, are more protected in your coupledom, and your relationship is safe.

- *What the Simple One can do.* Broaden your horizons, and try something new. The fact that you can recognize the problem of "simple" and "complicated" at all is an important sign for your relationship. It enters a new phase, the phase of transformation. You now have the chance to give a new depth to your relationship. Signal to your partner that you want to shape that new phase together. Tell your partner, "I'm happy that there's more there than I had thought." Build new spaces for yourself within your relationship, and invite the other in. Get interested in something new, develop yourself, transform yourself—do it somehow. You don't have to conquer the fields of interest and depth of your partner's soul—just go after your own at first. As long as your partner understands your new aspects, he or she will feel relieved and glad: "There's more in you than I thought there was."

- *What you both can do.* Learn from each other. The Simple One encourages you to be content and indicates how much good there already is between you. The Complicated One encourages growth and shows what all is still possible for the two of you. The good news is that in your homestead there are many more rooms than you think! There is room to add on, renovate, and expand; there are completely new, undiscovered regions. It's like a married farmer couple who turns their estate into an organic farm, starts a guesthouse, gets into energy production with rapeseed fields and biogas, or whatever. It's exciting and challenging, rewarding and risky.

It's the same way during your renovation and expansion phase. Each of you will sometimes feel insufficient and then sometimes superior, sometimes full of energy and then sometimes irritable. This can heavily burden your relationship. There will be moments again and again where you lose your faith in the great, shared project and wonder if it isn't better to go it alone.

Untangle Instead of Tearing. Resist these thoughts! Avoid an abrupt separation from your partner. It won't solve anything and will be the wrong kind of relief. Don't run blindly into another relationship. Don't send the other person off feeling hurt because you are painfully missing something. What you're looking for you can find above all in yourself.

Admit to your partner the unrest you're feeling. Give each other more room to search for your inner selves. Stay loyal to each other, "We are both looking for ourselves, and we won't hold each other back." Agree to continually talk about it, and allow each other to participate in the search. Reinforce your loyalty and your trust in your partner with clear language. Do so especially often and lovingly during this time. Your relationship will thus slowly expand and offer both of you more space. During the renovation phase of your homestead, it can still happen that the two of you lose touch in the construction site. Both develop further, but not necessarily in the same direction. So trade rooms again. Keep each other informed. Get into the craziness of the other, as strange and unusual as it may seem to you. Orient yourself according to the following rule: "We never know everything there is to know about our relationship, but it always offers enough space for learning more."

Maintain patiently the image of your large, magnificently expanded and renovated homestead in your mind. Orient yourself according to the motto: "Slowly disentangling is better than tearing." Even if it takes you a long time, you will avoid many frightening experiences in the dark forest.

The Fourth Dwelling of Love
The Dark Forest

Your Simplifying Dream: The Dark Forest

Up until now, you've awoken each time from the dream. But this dream is different. You long to wake up, you cry out for help, but you remain in the dark. You can feel that it has been daylight for some time now, but here under the deep, thick underbrush with tall greenish-black fir trees and strange broad-leaved plants above you no rays of light can penetrate. Trembling, you cower on the damp earth and try to remember where you are and how you got there.

Something drew you here—a power that you had never felt before yet seemed so familiar. You ask yourself, why did we have to build our magnificent homestead so close to this gloomy forest? For years you were hardly interested in the dark depths of the unknown woods directly behind your bedroom. You had even been warned about it. The two of you had gone in a little ways a few times, but didn't find anything interesting and quickly retreated from the bleak half-darkness of the giant trees and back into the sunny fields and meadows that you love so much.

But after some time, a feeling crept in that something was waiting for you out there, something you couldn't get at home. First, there was this slight feeling of discontent with your familiar life. This discontent didn't go away—it stayed and grew. It made you feel restless; it murmured inside of you, pushing, enticing, and pulling you away. You tried to ignore it, but a longing grew inside you. Though you didn't know where it would lead you or what you were looking for, you were ready to follow this feeling. Even if you had to throw all caution to the wind, you would go off into this wild forest to find out what it was—alone. The strange thing about it was that the person whom you loved and with whom you lived so comfortably seemed all the while distant and foreign. Your partner didn't even seem to notice when you started to make little trips into the dark forest. Then one day you disappeared into it, and there you now sit in the darkness.

So many couples wonder why a person even ends up at all in the dark forest with its gloomy shadows? Why can't we just enjoy our happy life in the homestead? Why do two people who love each other have arguments and stress, worry and misunderstandings, lies and estrangement?

The Feeling of Losing Yourself

Most people think that the reason for this is simple: the enchanting dreams in the love tent and the motivation that moved you into the homestead are gone, and routine sets in. Organizing a working schedule takes energy, and it doesn't exactly make you more passionate. Your energy for one another is directed toward your everyday tasks and that rejuvenating We loses its power. And so the question of the I comes back into the foreground.

Where am I? What happened to my tower, my freedom, and my self-sufficiency? These gnawing questions can make you unhappy because now you see your partner as an obstacle and an irritation. Fantasies develop about how much happier, simpler, and lighthearted your life would be without your partner. The things you could do if only you weren't tied to this person! Many couples have even learned to function under the extreme pressure of their many responsibilities. But their individual development was hindered. So they feel like they've come to a dead end, and they say, "I have to separate myself from you so I can be happy again." But that is the greatest error in the kingdom of love.

135

Don't Be Content with Mediocrity

This logic is a collective disconnect. Now it has its revenge when you've lost yourself in the homestead and adapted yourself completely to the We. When you can't work up the energy to develop yourself, a sense of mediocrity emerges in your relationship. You lose sight of the wonderful possibilities hiding inside you and your partner. Instead, you see only that, as people say, "There's nothing more in it for you guys. It happens to everyone. Just be content with your life and its limitations."

Then a terrible problem emerges: you're sick of being trapped, but think that the limitations you feel come from your partner. This is not surprising, since the collective opinion about the potential of a relationship is so negative. Usually people just shrug their shoulders and mention statistics about how many relationships fail. So every day, men and women fall into the trap of this unhealthy cycle and lose the person whom they love.

What Drives You into
the Dark Forest

The most important message we can give you as you enter the dark forest is that your journey into this forest isn't something to regret; rather, it is a necessary part of your personal journey through the kingdom of love. The thing that drives you into the darkness, loneliness, and confusion of this bizarre landscape of love is not the other person—even if it feels that way to you. The unrest and discontent come from inside of you. Your soul dreams of having a unique life. This is our great Western inheritance: each person should live the unique life that is laid out for him or her, one that no one else can live. C. G. Jung calls this driving force the "soul's desire for totality." This drive asks you to go for it all and not settle for comfortable compromises. It's powerful and demanding, but it's in no way an enemy of your relationship! On the contrary, your soul knows that you need support on your quest through the dark forest. It wants to look at your partner as an ally.

Being Alone Together

Through the tests of the dark forest, your soul practices becoming more empathetic, understanding, honest, courageous, and wise. Your soul has to manage this alone, and it won't always work right away. So your soul hopes that your beloved partner will allow it to go through these difficult trials within the protection of the relationship. No one is spared this journey, but you can assist one another by using the power of your relationship. You will make it through the dark forest easily because you aren't alone—even though you have to enter there alone.

Simplifying your love means focusing your gaze on love. See your love as being what supports you together, which is greater than you alone. Don't make your personal journey compete against your relationship. Allow each other to go forward without leaving the other behind. Remain allies. In the dark forest, your partnership will be put to the test, but it also gives you the strength to pass this test. You have sworn to stay together in good times and in bad. Now you have come upon difficult moments, the days of tests and trials. In this chapter, we want to help you make it through this journey as a person in a loving relationship.

Simplifying Idea 15: Wake Up

Many couples blindly run into the dark forest feeling mutual frustration because they don't understand the difference between an identity crisis and a relationship crisis. Usually, the identity crisis comes first.

If it's not recognized as such and instead blamed on the significant other, it turns into a relationship crisis, often with terrible consequences. With the following questions, you can test whether you or the relationship needs attention.

Identity Crisis or Relationship Crisis?

The feeling of inadequacy isn't necessarily an indication of a bad relationship or a sign of your own incapacity. Each person experiences this at some point. However, the blame for this inner dissatisfaction is quickly placed on the partner: "Because of you I can't . . ." Certainly,

there is always a reason for such an accusation, since the reality of a couple is so complicated that your identity formation has long been mixed with that of your partner's. But even if your partner plays a role, when things get tense between the two of you and you think of your partner as an obstacle to your development, you should always stop and look at yourself first.

Signs of an Identity Crisis. Which of the following sentences describe you?

- I'm leading a meaningless, average life.
- I don't want my life to continue the way it is now.
- I find my job boring./I'm unemployed.
- I feel worthless.
- I have problems in all areas, not only in my relationship.
- I feel isolated.
- I have anxiety about the future.
- I don't know what I really want.
- I often ask myself if this is all there is.
- I am actually a very different person.

If you've answered yes to one or more of these statements, then you're stuck in an "identity crisis." You're dealing with totally legitimate needs for personal development, which you've been pushing away, perhaps for the sake of your partner or your children or out of a strong need for security. By doing this, you are losing yourself. You should do the following right away to avoid having this become a relationship crisis.

- *Take responsibility.* Don't secretly blame your stagnation on or openly accuse your partner. Take immediate responsibility for your state of discontent, "It may have been completely OK until now, but I'm feeling that I need a change to continue being happy."
- *Trust your inner alarm clock.* Assume that the reason for your discontent lies within yourself. It's a wake-up call that your soul uses to motivate you into further development. This alarm-clock program is especially common during the midlife years between thirty-five and forty, or during times of transition (menopause, retirement, etc.). Such processes are labor intensive, but rewarding. They bring you personal maturity, emotional depth, and relaxed self-confidence.
- *Take the initiative.* Talk to your partner openly about your restlessness, "I want to change myself and develop in a positive way. You are very important to me, and you help keep me on track. I hope that our relationship also can benefit from my self-development."
- *Ask for support.* Ask your partner for his or her encouraging and loving companionship during this period. "All of this confusion and upheaval is not easy for me. And it certainly isn't easy for you, either. Please have patience with me."
- *Look at what connects you.* Be thankful for all the good that you have been able to create in this relationship. How has your partner already supported you? Tell your partner—the more explicitly, the better!

Indications of a Relationship Crisis. Which of the following sentences apply to you?

- I feel like I'm the one responsible for making this relationship work.
- My positive relationship signals aren't reaching my partner.
- I doubt that the other person is the right partner for me.
- I don't feel an erotic attraction between the two of us.
- I don't feel any emotional connection between the two of us.
- I don't feel any intellectual connection between the two of us.
- I can't fulfill the demands and wishes of my partner.
- We always just withdraw from one another and stop talking.
- We can only criticize and judge each other.

If you answered yes to one or more of these statements, then your relationship is having trouble. If you begin to punish your partner with shouting, angry criticism, cold withdrawal, or moodiness, you will provoke a true crisis. Your only solution is complete openness. You need to talk about the points to which you answered yes, and do so in a calm tone without accusations. In the following sections you will find helpful ideas and images to make it easier to start this conversation. Tell each other about your struggles, and talk about the dark figures that you've perhaps already encountered in the dark forest.

The Dragon: An Unavoidable Encounter . . .

When you investigate the dark forest more closely, you soon encounter a nightmarish dragon stirring trouble. You recognize this monster immediately, since it was one of the reasons why you gradually started feeling uncomfortable at home. This dragon is none other than your partner with all of his or her bad qualities. How could you have overlooked this terrible beast in the love tent? Ideally, you would like to throw something in its way and get out of there.

. . . Followed by an Even More Terrible One. But then more dragons appear, until you're finally standing in the dark forest face-to-face with your true enemy. It's not your partner's dragon—rather, it's your own. You know it by many names: your inner demon, the old patterns of behavior, your weaknesses . . . now you have it right before your eyes. It confronts you mercilessly amid your own darkness, and you can't run away from it.

Enmity with Yourself. What is this dragon good for? While the soul embodies your brightest and purest side, the dragon symbolizes the opposition of that: inward and outward hostility and destructiveness. When you have tracked the dragon down, there is an unmistakable sign that you have come very close not only to your ego, but also to your inner lost soul. The dragon is the adversary of your soul, but it also acts as a guardian.

Your dragon embodies your darkest qualities, a truth from which you usually shy away. You can go for years pretending that this dragon isn't there and instead point to your partner's very visible one. Psychologists call this repression and projection. But, your soul wants nothing more than for you to find your own monster and bravely confront it.

Tame Your Dragon . . . Say good-bye to the idea of conquering this monster in the dark forest by force. You will only hurt yourself. Approach your dragon without fear. Open your soul to loving images of transformation. Your dragon has the potential for this, just as in Michael Ende's children's book *Jim Button and the Wild 13*. In the end, the cruel dragon Mrs. Grindtooth becomes a Golden Dragon of Wisdom.

. . . and Embrace Your Partner's. Don't be afraid of your partner's dragon anymore. Poet Rainer Maria Rilke suggested that "Perhaps all the dragons in our lives are princesses who are only waiting to see us act, just once, with beauty and courage." Precisely this terrible side of

us is "in its deepest essence, something helpless that wants our help." Rush to help your partner's dragon by feeding it loving understanding so that it remembers its good soul and becomes calm and peaceful.

The following is a list of dragons, some of which are familiar to you. But only one of them is the real guardian of your soul, harassing it terribly. Read through all nine descriptions, and then look more carefully at the two types that are closest to yours and your partner's.

- *The raging fire-breather.* For long periods of time, its behavior is very controlled and disciplined. In some sense, it is an exemplary dragon, but at times its violent inner fire can erupt like a volcano. It showers you with guilt, bitter

accusations, and caustic criticism. It does this unconsciously because it has kept itself under control, but this self-control doesn't lead to better quality of life for its soul. This pain burns inside of it like a consuming fire, which is then hurled at others because of its great frustration.

  How to tame your dragon: Get used to the idea that you are also aggressive. Feed your inner dragon with lots of goodness, patience, and humor. Don't continuously tie yourself down with your strict sense of obligation. Take comfort in nature. Allow yourself light, playful moments. Life isn't only serious—it's also cheerful!

- *The giant slimy dragon of pride.* At first glance, this dragon doesn't seem terrible at all; it is more like an affectionate pet. It likes to appear modest, but it knows exactly how indispensable its help is. It thinks no one could support the soul as well as it can. No one would take such good care of its mistress as it does. It is proud because it is so important to her. It wants to be fed this acknowledgment; otherwise, it becomes deeply offended. This pain in its dragon heart reveals how dependent it really is on others.

How to tame your dragon: Help your dragon gain more freedom. Don't hound at your partner's heels so closely. Your relationship needs more air; your partner and your children don't need as much constant attention as you think. Don't manipulate others with favors. Give yourself freely. You just need to take more time to do what makes you happy.

■ *The tricky sparkler.* This dynamic dragon has won many Oscars—or at least it says it has. This dragon brightens up its image and status with public appeal to be recognized as a high-powered blaze of a dragon. This savvy tactician can slip into many different roles. It bluffs, deceives, and cheats. It has the look of a winner and enchants others with the power of its words. To succeed, this dragon bends the truth and skates over its own and others' feelings. It confuses admiration with love, and it doesn't only deceive others, but above all it deceives itself. This dragon, however, doesn't feel the greatest pain: that it's not brave enough to be totally upfront and honest with itself.

How to tame your dragon: Surround yourself and your inner dragon with a few honest people who can tell you the truth. Practice looking inside of you, digging out and communicating your true feelings. Do good without talking about it or trying to gain something by it.

- *The envious, sorrowful lizard.* This dazzlingly extravagant and often morose dragon tends to have extreme mood swings and easily feels as if someone has stepped on its tail. Insensitive words irritate it. This dragon thinks of itself as the one true guardian of the treasure, the one who really knows the needs of its soul. It doesn't get along well with other dragons. They are too coarse for it, too dumb, and too ordinary. But secretly, it is consumed with envy by the beautiful towers, tents, and homesteads of others. It doesn't understand why  others have so much beauty and happiness, while it has the worse fate, despite a fine sense of what is genuine and noble. Its great pain is not being able to balance its own feelings.

  How to tame your dragon: Get rid of all the special treatment for this delicately nerved animal. Go for simplicity and plainness. This supports inner balance. Inner strength also requires the power of the ordinary—the ability to share a normal day with a normal partner.

- *The greedy, hoarding dragon.* This quiet loner is withdrawn and lives in its cool grotto. You hardly see it before it disappears again. This dragon hates spontaneity. If you come too close, you'll be enveloped by a fog of Latin. It anxiously hordes its treasure of knowledge, doesn't like to share its time with others, digs into its books, and is careful not to show its emotions. The greatest passion of this dragon is gathering information, and it's insatiable. The gnawing pain 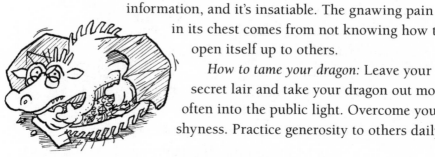 in its chest comes from not knowing how to open itself up to others.

  How to tame your dragon: Leave your secret lair and take your dragon out more often into the public light. Overcome your shyness. Practice generosity to others daily.

Dare to express your deep feelings. Invite other people in, and take on the role of the generous host.

- *The mistrustful scaredy-dragon.* This dragon always smells an attack and is extremely watchful, always on guard, and full of mistrust. Overly cautious, it warns the soul about things that clearly are harmless, which it has made into bigger threats. This dragon spreads conspiracy theories and sees enemies everywhere. Nothing is certain; it doesn't really even trust itself. It always hides its chicken heart behind threatening gestures and sudden, unexpected attacks. This dragon is tortured by self-doubt, condemning it to longing for some kind of authority, which it must then once again distrust.

  How to tame your dragon: Use your skill of clever planning and organize an antifear program. Make a decision and stick to it, name three things that went well today, and bolster others and show your trust in them. Think of the world as conspiring to do you good!

- *The insatiable pleasure dragon.* This vagabond changes position with lightning speed and pops up wherever there's something to be gained. It doesn't like real dragon battles; it would rather avoid the danger zone through its clever maneuvers. Driven by its insatiable need for amusing experiences or endeavors, it circles restlessly high above the ground. This way, it overcomes all of the limitations that others place on themselves. As this dragon flies high, it pounces upon anything that moves and gorges on anything interesting that crosses its path. For this pleasure-seeking creature, the painful spot is locked up and covers the fear of the emptiness that haunts it.

How to tame your dragon: Pull your inner dragon down, firmly grounding it in reality. Reduce its and your activities. Don't follow every impulse. Less is more! Look more closely into your relationship; your partner deserves some quiet time. Send yourself into the quiet, so that you can find and scoop yourself out of the depths.

- *The shameless destroyer-dragon.* This wingless dragon, bristling with power, can crush anything in its way without a thought. When it angrily lashes about, trying to protect its poor little soul, it doesn't even see all that it is destroying. This dragon carelessly prevails with the right of the strong. It remembers every slight and revenges itself by mercilessly exposing the weaknesses of its opponents. This dragon shows no  feelings of shame. Its tortuous pain lies in its inability to find someone equal to it, who approaches it without fear and can bear its full brunt.

  How to tame your dragon: Find something small and tender that you can care for—a child, an animal, or a flower. This helps you access your sensitivity, from which your power draws its energy. Respect the boundaries of your partner. Don't expect so much from yourself or others. Through tender words and mild gestures, let your power flow into your relationship.

- *The yawning lazy-bones dragon.* Sometimes you'll find this wingless dragon slumped like a heavy sack on the forest floor, hardly moving, and sleeping while others work for its comfort. With its enormous size, it can bullishly refuse to do something, spread boredom, see the sense in doing nothing, and pass off its listlessness as tranquillity. When this dragon makes itself idly comfortable, resignation, passivity, and indifference spread quickly around it. Especially ruinous is its undemanding nature, which can suffocate enthusiasm as soon as it starts. The hidden pain in its poor dragon heart is that it doesn't know how to unfold its talents; so it can't work toward a goal.

How to tame your dragon: Help your dragon onto its feet, and say good-bye to its laziness. Don't have others do things for you; rather, take the initiative yourself. Marvel at what powers this awakens in you. Give yourself small relationship tasks everyday, which you can take care of quickly. Gradually entrust yourself to larger and larger responsibilities.

The Robber's Cave: Oppressive Scarcity

Deep in the dark forest, the robber's cave lies in a shadowy canyon. This is where you end up when your relationship lacks respect and equality. One of you has taken on the more powerful position of the robber, while the other has the weaker position of the poor victim.

The robber's cave is often symbolic of the woman's experience. She has taken a break from her career or cut back on her hours, and now she bears the brunt of the housework. Feelings of frustration, powerlessness, and insignificance grow within her. She used to be free, but now she is financially dependent and locked out of life. She feels that her partner has robbed her of her profes-sional development, of her hopes and dreams, and of her best years. To her, the relationship feels like a dead end, like a prison. She is afraid of the threatening stagna-tion and transfers this existential anxiety onto him. He is the actual threat, and she's at his mercy.

Recognize the Symptoms of Powerlessness. As the robber's victim, you feel like that egotist is to blame for all of your misery. He can have his career, move about freely, and come and go as he pleases. You feel tied to family and household, caring for younger and older family members. Women see their home as a place where something always needs to be done so others can feel comfortable and taken care of. Perhaps you also saw your mother's life this way. Sometimes you expect your partner to also do things around the house. If he doesn't do it, he becomes a self-obsessed bum in your eyes who doesn't worry about anything, patronizes you, exploits you, and on top of it all, wants you to clean "his cave." He controls how much money you spend, but he does whatever he wants with it. You find your partner insensitive and rude. You see yourself as undervalued, shut out, lost, and alone. Your everyday life is uncomfortable, the tone of your voice is harsh, your feelings have cooled, and the mood is now icy. The reason behind this is that you didn't leave yourself access to the outside world, and now you can't sufficiently fight for your own autonomy.

The danger that grows is that at some point you will heedlessly break out to escape the dismal life in the cold robber's cave. In the worst-case scenario, you'll run off with the next bandit who comes by. Then what was in your imagination ("My relationship feels like a robber's cave.") becomes reality: you're off with someone else, who in the eyes of your husband is the worst robber of all—an evil blackguard who stole his wife and the mother of his children.

Ways out of the Robber's Cave. A successful way out of the robber's cave involves going outside and taking some time for yourself.

- *Let go of the victim role.* Think of what you have done (or not done) and how your potential has gone unrealized. Believe that you can positively transform your situation yourself. Be brave and take the initiative.
- *Stand up straight and confident beside your partner.* Explain that this situation is not acceptable for you. Name three concrete, objective, and understandable reasons as to why you feel

inferior. Then make three concrete suggestions for what you want to immediately change, both in the short term and in the long term. Be a tough negotiator, but patient and fair. Agree to make all important decisions together.

■ *Rethink how you control your shared finances.* Whoever controls the money usually also has more power in the relationship. Work this out either through equal access to your financial means (if both of you are responsible with money) or through firm agreement on how to manage your finances so that you have enough and you don't need to continuously fight about money (when you have debts).

■ *Make yourself room to move about.* You need set windows of time when you can also come and go and do as you please. Recognize your need for "me time," and tell your partner the number of hours per week that you need for yourself. During this time, he must be responsible for the children.

■ *Recognize your own robber side.* Retract unfair projections or accusations of guilt. Consciously avoid secret robberlike tendencies: intrigue, money hoarding, patronizing, unscrupulous behavior, and other unfair claims for power or possessions.

■ *See the love.* See that your supposed robber is actually the person who loves you and stands by you. Praise him as the good partner who doesn't want to exploit or oppress you. Thank him for his loyalty to his family and his bravery for working to provide for the family. Create closeness between you so that warmth can start flowing again. What form of respect would fill him with pride?

The Witch's House: Oppressive Demands

In a different part of the dark forest stands the house of a crooked witch. You end up here when your relationship is missing honesty and empathy. In the witch's house are evil magic potions made from meanness, bitter accusations, and twisted truths. Like a slow poison, it eats away at your relationship. Here you have all the secret recipes for emotionally attacking your partner.

In everyday life, men often have the staggering feeling of having let themselves be coaxed into the witch's house. Instead of warmth and affection, the witch's kitchen only dispenses bad moods and griping. From the man's perspective, his partner isn't only moody and cranky like an old witch, but she also poisons the atmosphere and instills fear within him and the children. Because she constantly criticizes, questions, and belittles him, his home is no longer a refuge from his life at work. Instead, he is confronted with demands and showered with reproaches. In this situation, a man feels that his partner is a demanding witch who always asks too much of him, loading him up with more tasks, wanting more time and money, while trying to gain more power over him.

Recognize the Symptoms of Your Poisoning. You suffer from the daily nagging and complaining that awaits you at home. You feel worn out from the burden of all of these demands. You have the feeling that you can never satisfy your partner. You can't get rid of the feeling of being a failure or that you owe her something. Despite what you do, she is so intuitive that she will surely discover your next weakness even before you do. You are sick of always being attacked and ridiculed. You're often in a dark mood, getting grumpier, more irritable, and more discontent. The reason behind this is you have neglected your own emotional side, and you have a hard time determining your feelings and putting them into words.

Ways out of the Witch's House. You will find your way out of the dilemma of the witch's house when you are conscious of all of your feelings.

- *Bring light into the darkness of the witch's house.* Throw the windows open inside of you; stand up and say to yourself that you shouldn't be afraid of the accusations. Tell your partner how much you suffer from her bad moods when at home. Always ask to address only one accusation at a time. In a confrontational climate, accusations are often blown out of proportion, although they usually contain a kernel of truth. Concentrate on getting to this kernel. Ask your partner if this point summarizes the issue. If not, she should formulate the kernel clearly and precisely. If it clicks with you, then you can acknowledge this one point as a disturbing factor in your relationship and work out a solution together.

- *Show some heart.* Don't hide your feelings behind the mask of a rationalist who is above his feelings. Give your partner the chance to look into your heart, and ask her to do the same. Stay in this position until you can feel something new. Practice looking at your feelings every day; practice interpreting them and dealing with them. Adhere to the following rule: "You don't need to apologize for your feelings. But you're responsible for how you deal with them."

- *Do a Mommy-check.* Check whether you're projecting the darker aspects of your mother's image onto your wife. Take C. G. Jung's warning seriously: "Every obstacle that rises in a man's path and hampers his ascent wears the shadowy features of the Terrible Mother, who saps his strength with the poison of secret doubt and retrospective longing." Are you irritated because "life" or your partner doesn't "just" give you everything you want? Overcome this desire; be an adult and create your own warmth and care. By doing this, you'll gain back the smiling love of your wife.

■ *Recognize your own witch side.* Take back unjustified accusations of guilt or projections. Consciously avoid taunting, curses, irritability, trickery, deceitfulness, untruths, pickiness, and emotional coldness.

■ *See the love.* Recognize that your supposed witch is the woman who shares in all of your feelings and thoughts. With her talent for understanding emotional depth, your partner can help you unlock the richness of your own emotions. Thank her for reacting so sensitively to inconsistencies that call attention to problems in the relationship. What form of your affection would make her happy?

Simplifying Idea 16:
Do Fight—but Fight Fair

"You have to also be able to fight"—this is a well-meaning piece of advice from commonsense psychology. But in this abbreviated form, it's dangerous. Now and then, an isolated quarrel isn't bad; a good relationship can hold the opposite poles of attraction and rejection together. But when the negative energies take control of a couple's behavior and communication, the couple drifts apart. This is why we start this section with conflict, which is the worst danger for your relationship and can arise out of your daily corrosive skirmishes.

The Four Horsemen of the Apocalypse in Your Relationship

Your relationship is threatened by four patterns of behavior that the couples researcher John Gottman has called the "four horsemen of the apocalypse" after Albrecht Dürer's woodcut (even though Gottman's horsemen don't really have anything to do with these four figures from the Book of Revelations). They are among the greatest risk factors in a relationship, as they chase a couple deep into the dark forest and sabotage all your positive perceptions of each other. In the worst-case scenario, these four horsemen can ruin a relationship.

First Horseman: Criticism. Criticism consists of grip-ing, nagging, accusing, and attacking that goes beyond the situation and is directed person-ally against the partner, generally denigrating him or her: "You're always so uptight," "You never have time," "You drive me crazy with your perpetual mess." Above all, this strat-egy is used by women, who don't realize how much they break down their partner's trust by doing so. Often these accusations do come from accurate observations, but over the course of the years this behavior has turned into an unhealthy pattern: you focus only on imperfections and your own negative feelings. This poisons not only your surround-ings, but also yourself.

Second Horseman: Scorn, Disdain, and Disrespect. You once fell in love with each other because you both admired one another. Now this reverence for the other person has receded or disappeared altogether. Instead you make deprecating com-ments, suspect your partner of evil intentions, hurt your partner consciously or unconsciously, insult him or her, and pull your partner apart in front of others. In the end, you judge your partner: "Well, we can't expect anything else from a failure like you."

Third Horseman: Defensiveness. At the beginning of a relationship, you let the other person tell you when you've done something wrong.

Later, this decreases drastically. You justify yourself and deny your own part in conflicts. You live according to the motto: "I'm the victim, and you're the one doing something wrong. It's all your fault that I'm so unhappy, and so I have to counterattack: You're the problem, not me."

Fourth Horseman: Walls. You block yourself off, don't react anymore, are indifferent and cold, and in the end pull away completely—emotionally or physically—by not being around very much. In 85 percent of such cases, it's the man who pulls the shades, leaves the room, or seems to fall emotionally silent. Women feel that this behavior is extremely hurtful.

How to Defend Against the Four Horsemen. Now and then, these four horsemen gallop through the dark forest, even in happy relationships. But happy couples are capable of resisting the horsemen's long-term siege on the homestead. Learn the two most effective weapons against them:

- *Timely intervention.* There will be some nagging, disrespect, denial, and shutting off in every relationship. And even in seemingly war-torn relationships, there are always peace offerings: "I do still love you," "I'm so happy that I have you." The difference is that in bad marriages, the couple overlook these peace offerings, but in good marriages, they take them to heart. Gottman's long-term studies have shown that in more than 80 percent of marriages that ended in divorce, the husbands have ignored their wives' peace offerings. Fifty percent of the wives didn't notice those of their husbands. In good relationships, the number was only 19 percent (men) and 14 percent (women). Use this simplifying rule: in times of quarrel and crisis, send more positive messages (Gottman recommends five positive statements for every negative one) and respond to each positive signal from your partner.

- *A good look back.* Ninety-four percent of couples who describe their past together also expect a happy future. Unhappy couples, on the other hand, concentrate on each other's mistakes. Like proverbial elephants, they never forget these mistakes, but they also don't remember the good times in their relationships. Here is a simplifying rule: each of you should preserve the pleasant details of your love story like treasures in your heart and in your memory. These are really quite effective morsels. Write down all of this goodness, possibly even together, and add new happy moments regularly.

Precautions Against Escalation

How can you carry these insights over into everyday life? We recommend (just like with physical wellness) an ironclad prevention program. During "peacetime," come to agreement on the following rules, whose bright light of friendly interaction might seem a little strange to you. But when bad weather comes, these rules can really make a difference. Promise each other not to discuss these rules during a confrontation, but to just follow them. Just as a country has a constitution, you have your firm rules of conflict, which set limits on the argument.

Agree to a Time Limit. It sounds crazy, but it works. Decide that an argument can never last more than fifteen minutes. In most cases, everything necessary is said by then anyway. If it goes on longer, old grievances come out, and the healing confrontation gives way to trench warfare, which injures and exhausts both parties. It is important to realize that men take longer to calm down after a fight than women do, because their stress level decreases more slowly. For them, this time limit is even more important because a clear stopping point helps them to stay

put. During these fifteen minutes, neither person is allowed to leave. After fifteen minutes, though, you may go as the time is up. After this quarter-hour, do something that eases your mind: listen to music, get some fresh air, or do some housework.

No Flight Scenes. If one of you makes a rude, hurtful, mean, or reproachful comment and the other protests, neither of you may leave the room. It can become a terrible habit that one person pulls the pin on a psychological hand grenade, tosses it into the room, and then flees while its devastating effects take hold in the other person's heart. The rules of engagement between the two of you include that no one gets to run away. When something happens, it's time-out—everything freezes, and it's time to talk. The conversation doesn't have to last long. But when the communication in your relationship collapses, things soon look very, very bleak.

Limit the Battlefield. Right at the start of the conflict, clarify the issue: What are we dealing with right now, at this moment? What exactly happened? Is it worth fighting about? Was it maybe just a glitch, a foul? Who admits guilt? Can we be good sports about it? If not, when should we talk about this in detail?

Reconcile halfway: what just happened has been named and is no longer an issue. Strengthen this with a gesture (a hug, a kiss). This will keep every little thing from turning into a huge explosion. Look at it like an attorney: when the issue of the claim is too small, no suit is brought.

Agree not to open up any old archives. Couples have an elephant's memory for failed conversations. Make a new beginning with your confrontations: "We often used to be nasty in fights. But we're getting better at it all the time."

Cultivate a Good Tone. In your communication with your partner, on principle avoid all swearwords, sarcastic humor, possibly irony—even when you're not arguing. Humor itself is good, but remember that the healthiest laughter is laughter at yourself. Always include yourself in your jokes. This defuses touchy situations quickly—especially if your partner likes to weigh every word.

Be Realistic. During a good, argument-free phase, ask yourselves, how good is our relationship? Compare it with other relationships—your parents', friends', maybe even celebrities'. You'll find that your relationship isn't all that bad. No one can have a prize-winning "model" marriage. Congratulate yourselves for having found each other. Bury the fantasy that the grass is always greener on the other side.

Don't Gather Ammunition. When you're irritated at your partner about something little or something big, express it lovingly but as soon as possible. Love should remain your top priority. Think to yourself: "I'm telling you this because I love you, and I'm saying it in a way that you can hear my love." Don't store up ammunition for later and then bury your partner in all of your stored-up anger from the last few days and overwhelm him or her.

Give Your Conversation a Good Start. Begin your conversation calmly. If your partner wants to talk to you in the evening, you can ask to take a pause first to charge up your "listening" battery. This is done best by going for a walk alone, listening to music, or reading quietly. But agree beforehand on a time when you should be ready to talk and to listen. Otherwise, your desire for quiet time will be taken as, "I don't want to talk to you."

Listen Intelligently. Social researcher Larry Barker has discovered an unusual human ability: when you act like you're listening, you soon actually start to listen. Look at your partner often (without staring), nod frequently, make agreeing sounds, smile encouragingly, change your position and facial expression—and your actual attention and sympathy for the other person will increase. Don't let yourself get distracted by looking somewhere else or reacting too much to outside noises. This can be insulting and lead to a long-lasting break in the conversation.

Asking questions, making comments, or even adding just little corrections ("That was 1991, not 1990") can permanently sabotage a conversation. When the other is searching for words, let him or her search. When your partner is silent, bear that silence. Endure incorrect details or what you think are false judgments. Instead, repeat every now and then what the other person said.

Be Near Each Other. The more touchy a subject is, the more sensitive a person becomes. A person doesn't only need to feel that the other is listening, but also to be certain that he or she is not being judged or worse, condemned. As soon as your partner starts to talk about something he or she is ashamed of, you should do more than be neutral and still. A good "cuddle position" makes this  easier. When you have difficult conversations, sit on the sofa, light a candle, look at each other, and touch or put your arms around each other. This makes it clear that, "Whatever you say, I am with you. Whatever is bothering you, it's not going to take me away from you." Always sit close enough together so you can touch, hold, or embrace when it's appropriate.

Show Your Anger in the First Person. Practice the art of the gentle confrontation. Say what bothers you, but stay on topic and stick to your feelings. Criticize the action, not the person. Avoid generalizations and put-downs. Something to note: start each sentence with *I*, because these sentences don't turn into accusations as often as the ones that start out with *you*. If your partner has forgotten an appointment or commitment, say, "I'm really sad that I had to go there alone tonight," and not "You never pay attention to my appointments, because you only think about yourself." Also watch out for roundabout accusations: for example, if you say "you women," your partner will hear this as an attack on her.

Allow for Compensation. When you get upset about some detail ("He never does the dishes"), think of a positive detail about your partner at the same time ("He has our finances under control"). When your partner has messed something up, give him or her a chance to fix it without losing face.

Celebrate Reconciliation. Accept a white flag. Pay careful attention to your partner's peace offerings. If the other person lets you know that he or she doesn't want to fight anymore, then stop. Enjoy your victory quietly, even if it's only a small one, but resist the temptation to keep humiliating the loser.

If an argument goes on too long, start by making yourself admit a weakness. Don't do it whiningly or submissively, but rather directly, as one of two equal adults. Acknowledge your part in the argument. Praise something about your partner's behavior. Offer a way to make up for something you've done. The further in the past an issue is, the more important it is to let go of the argument and to forgive.

If forgiveness is generally difficult for you, then think of a person who can be your role model in forgiving. Forgiveness has nothing to do with weakness. It expresses the sovereignty in your ability to let go of injuries. Preserve your own dignity, and don't allow yourself to be hurt by your partner in this way again.

When you have made it through a really difficult situation together, you can celebrate with a small thanksgiving in recognition of it. As the two "survivors," you can praise the heroism of this relationship achievement together. For example, you could place a good symbol in a corner of your home to remind you of your heroic deed. Or buy yourselves new wedding rings.

No Physical Violence. Never. Nor any implied violence, not even verbal mentions of violence ("I'd like to just smack you"). This is in the first place a tip for men, but women also use aggressive behavior. If it gets to this point, you can forget the actual topic of your conversation, because now it's only about aggression.

Therefore, end the conversation if one of you gets aggressive. Explain clearly that you can't talk anymore, and ask your partner to end the conversation. Set up a time together, and take the initiative yourself to continue the conversation in a calmer mood.

If the argument is unavoidable, preserve the peace. Even if you get loud, you can stay fair. Your opponent is the person whom you love, not your enemy.

When the Conflict Won't Go Away

In cases of long-lasting conflict, seek professional help before your relationship gets into a crisis that can't be overcome. But where do you find this kind of support? In every large city, there are counseling centers you can turn to. Religious centers also offer this kind of counseling. Larger cities have spiritual guidance refuges where you can get a trustworthy referral.

How to Find a Helper Who Really Helps. One often overlooked source is your family doctor. A relationship crisis often includes physical symptoms (e.g., hearing loss, tinnitus, migraines, chest pains, back pain), and when such symptoms are present, insurance companies will often pay for psychotherapy. What many people don't know is that you can go to any psychoanalyst or psychotherapist for a "trial run." Look for providers with special training in relationship therapy. Don't be afraid to ask openly. Beforehand, clarify whether your insurance

is accepted. The costs of the first few sessions will certainly be covered. Use these trial sessions to find out whether you have a good connection with the therapist and feel understood and taken seriously.

In the Devil's Canyon: Domestic Abuse

If physical violence is frequent in your relationship, you stand on an especially dangerous cliff in the dark forest. On the edge of the devil's canyon, your life can be in danger. "Domestic violence," as it is officially known, can happen in every family. It's independent of income, education, social status, or age. Ninety-five percent of the time it's committed by the man, is repeated regularly, and gets progressively worse.

The main dilemma is that abusers are often socially isolated and try to isolate their wife and children. They can't handle negative feelings, don't allow discussions, or try to end them with some expression of power. When they don't achieve anything that way, their rage turns into violence. Very often, alcohol plays a role.

Leave the Devil's Canyon Immediately. Don't hope for better times. A vicious circle starts when the causes aren't changed: an outburst is followed by reconciliation and then a period of renewed intimacy, which keeps the woman from leaving. After a short while, it starts over from the beginning, sometimes over years. That's why violence in a relationship requires immediate professional help from outside! Together or on your own, turn to a family counseling center. This is your last chance. There they can offer you special training programs or protection.

Make a Safety Plan. It's important for you to look ahead and know how you can protect yourself and your children in an emergency. Many organizations and family centers have collected tips on their websites for women in danger.

- *Turn to neighbors or friends.* Don't be too ashamed to inform others about your threatening situation. Create an emergency program together so that everyone knows exactly what they have to do. Get the address of the nearest women's shelter. Make copies of your personal documents, bank statements, and your address book. Add to that some cash, a second key for your home and car, as well as some basic clothing for a few days. Leave this all with a person you trust and to whom you can go if you suddenly have to leave your home.
- *Prepare your children.* Tell your children that violence is always wrong, even when it's someone close to you. For safety's sake, your children should always stay out of the way

during an altercation. Agree on a code word that the children understand as a sign to leave the house and get help. Make sure they know the number 911. Think about escape routes and practice leaving the house quickly with your children. In moments of danger, yell "Fire!" instead of "Help!" Experience shows that neighbors or passersby will react quicker and can step in.

■ *Avoid threatening situations.* Don't aggravate an argument with emotional accusations. Set limits, but don't provoke your partner. The more degraded he feels emotionally, the sooner he will try to win back control through the use of force. In an argument, avoid the kitchen at all costs—too many objects there could become weapons on the spur of the moment. Leave the house the moment you feel threatened.

■ *Seek professional help.* There is a women's hotline in almost every city, and the number should be in the front of the phone book. The telephone is the best resource here. For security reasons, addresses of safe houses for women are not published, but only given to women who need them.

Simplifying Idea 17: Defend Your Relationship

Your partnership (like every happiness) needs to be protected not only against internal threats, but also against enemies attacking from the outside. The most dangerous opponents, according to the astounding results of the studies by John Gottmann, are

■ Jealousy (of an opponent who might not even exist)
■ A third person with whom your partner falls in love (and who is quite real)
■ The clan (e.g., a mother-in-law)

In addition, there are threats from bad advisers, as well as economic problems, illnesses, and unemployment, which don't actually attack the couple itself, but are commonly the cause for divorce.

You can and should defend yourself against these potential enemies of your relationship, and you should do it smartly, in a timely manner, and as united as you can.

Decide Against Jealousy

The realization comes slowly, but usually with great force; you realize that your partner considers you as his or her own personal possession. Or you are plagued by the fear of losing the affection of the person you love. Jealousy can affect anyone—the victim as well as the perpetrator. But you're not as helpless in the face of this powerful emotion as it may sometimes seem.

Forget Rational Explanations. Jealousy is the fear of loss within a triangular situation consisting of three people. A jealous person is pulled back and forth between love and hate; he or she is afraid of losing the loved one and paradoxically starts to hate that person. This is actually a contradiction. Jealousy isn't about facts, but rather about perceptions.

There is no rational explanation hiding behind jealousy, even if it sometimes seems to the jealous person as if he or she is seeing everything quite clearly. In reality that's precisely what the person is not doing. Many relationships fail because the jealous person can't trust his or her partner and can't just enjoy the partner's presence. Through mistrust, the jealous person destroys the relationship.

Recognize the Warning Signs. Jealousy is tied to a mixture of very different feelings: fear, anger, powerlessness, shame, and sadness. Physical symptoms can also play a role. To be jealous is to double-doubt; a jealous person doubts and puts down him- or herself (e.g., "I'm not as worthy of love, as attractive, as smart as . . ."). In addition, the jealous person doubts and mistrusts the other person, as well as suspects him or her of something negative, disrespecting the person in the process.

When you are jealous, you want to have your beloved all to yourself. You make scenes, spy on your partner, and rifle through his or her things and private spaces. You search your partner's words for "hints" that something's going on. The ominous thing about this is that the less concrete evidence you find, the more you imagine your worst fears are coming true.

Antidote: consciously enjoy the presence of your partner and don't burden him or her with suspicions. Picture your partner's positive side, and tell your partner what you like about him or her. This will decrease your own desire to control your partner.

Reveal Your Shadows. Jealousy of an imaginary rival is a so-called relief-projection. You push away your own feeling of low self-worth and attribute it to your rival. This way, you don't have to confront your own negative side, and you feel better for the short term. In the long term, though, you block important growth processes—such as the insight into how worthy of love you can be, despite all of your weaknesses and mistakes.

Antidote: admit your jealousy. Bring it out of the darkness of your unconscious into the light of your conscious awareness. Have a written conversation with your jealousy: "Why are you here? What do I have to do to get rid of you?" Show your jealousy the suffering that it causes you and others. After every sentence, let your jealousy answer—also in writing. This method of "active imagination" has proven very useful in revealing self-deception.

Discover the Freedom of Your Relationship. You have so much fear of being left, because you draw your self-esteem from your relationship with your partner. Only here do you feel loved and accepted. You need the other person's presence and constant confirmations. This is exactly what annoys your partner. Instead of love, your partner experiences control and pressure. This can lead to your partner actually seeking distance or even separation. Then your jealousy will have won: what you at first only imagined would become a reality.

Antidote: don't imagine your relationship as a room in which you always have to be together. Remember that your homestead is a house with many rooms: living rooms and bedrooms for the intimacy of your relationship, as well as a room for each of you alone for the intimacy of your own development. These rooms are your future workshops, in which each can move forward with him- or herself. Both have connecting doors into the couple's room. This way you can encounter each other as equals and consciously as a couple.

Detach Yourself from Your Jealousy. You may be jealous, but you aren't your jealousy. It is a program running inside of you, a cluster of feelings that are sometimes like a sickness—and like a sickness, they can also subside.

Antidote: think of your jealousy as a difficult employee who you can send out to take a walk. You are the boss. Make the jealousy go plague whom it will, but for the moment, it has to be gone for two hours. If it pops back up during this time, then it has no business here. Increase this program until you can send your jealousy on vacation for several weeks at a time.

At some point, you should finally let go and officially fire it.

Among the Poachers: Infidelity

Many dark factors can heavily burden your relationship. You live in different places (i.e., a long-distance relationship); you don't get emotionally and physically close enough; you talk without passion or empathy for each other; you don't express your needs, longings, and dreams; or you feel disrespected, ignored, unacknowledged, or emotionally unsupported by your partner. Most of these things are communication problems, which gradually bring serious shortcomings into your relationship: too little feeling, too little understanding, too little sex. If you don't do anything about these things that are lacking, then you end up in a vacuum. This attracts a third party from the outside, who fills this empty space again. Statistics show that this third party usually comes from your circle of friends or your work environment and is usually in a committed relationship of his or her own. With this person, your system seems energetically complete again. But it is in no way intact.

Having an Affair: The Fatal Risk for Your Relationship. Forget all of the popular fairy tales and romance about having an affair. Even if many people do it, it isn't necessarily a good thing. An affair is the worst threat for your relationship. It is the extreme opposite of simplifying your love. Our simplifying advice in this matter is very simple: don't do it!

Many people consider an affair as sufficient grounds for immediately ending the relationship, even with all of the terrible consequences that accompanies it: separation or divorce; a financial catastrophe; and damage to your children, your circle of friends, and your professional reputation. A separation costs you an incredible amount of time and psychological energy, and it even lowers your life expectancy. Even if you are able to build up another relationship after a divorce, the new relationship will be burdened by the previous one for a long time.

If a couple can manage to start over after one partner has had an affair, the relationship still suffers for a long time. Studies conducted by Germany's leading expert on extramarital affairs, Ragnar Beer, show clearly that the injuries the betrayal causes in the emotional world of the betrayed person are awful. They only very, very slowly subside and even years later are not completely gone. A later divorce is often related to the difficulty of rebuilding trust.

Ragnar Beer summarizes the startlingly clear results of his ten-year study in serious terms:

Extramarital affairs are one of the worst things that can happen to a relationship. The unfaithful partner can't miss the manifold consequences that the cover-up, bad conscience, doubt in the relationship, or an unwanted new love bring with them. If people knew what anger and what suffering their affair would cause themselves and their partner, most would forget it all together and invest their energy in the relationship instead.

How You Both Can Avoid an Affair. The best thing to do is to consider a third party attempting to intrude on your relationship as a threatening poacher in the dark forest. If you both protect yourselves in a timely way, this person can't push his or her way between you. Hence the following preventive measures:

- *Take troubles seriously.* Even if they seem unfounded, the complaints of your partner and his or her anger, frustration, or worry should never just be wiped off the table. If they're not expressed, you'll find yourselves arguing again and again—or shutting off altogether. Speaking is living; silence is death. If you can't find a good solution that you are both comfortable with, then the danger of an affair comes closer.
- *Don't monitor each other.* And this means neither emotionally nor materially. Don't treat each other like your own property. The miracle of love only happens when it can flow on its own. As soon as one of you slides into a bad position or always has to take the backseat, you become open to external influences.
- *Examine your feelings for a third party.* Be radically honest with yourself when something sparks inside of you. What does this signal tell you about your relationship? What exactly is this feeling? (E.g., "I find this person unbelievably attractive, because she radiates such positive energy.") Trace this feeling back to its origin. Where does this feeling root from inside of you? Where does it come from? This is much more important than chasing after it to see where it will lead— and lead you astray. How can this feeling of something missing in your relationship

bring you closer to yourself? A feeling whose message you've understood can always be used to do something good for your relationship.

■ *Change your sex life.* In about 80 percent of cases, sexual discontent is the reason for having an affair. Talk to each other about your unfulfilled wishes in bed. Ragnar Beer has discovered that couples don't need to suffer as much as they do because of their unfulfilled sexual desires. Most people who were questioned would have liked to fulfill their partner's wishes—if they only knew what those wishes were! The only way to discover unknown desires in your relationship is to talk about what you're longing for. You will get it more easily than you expect and can thus avoid extramarital affairs.

How to Protect Yourself from Temptation. If your relationship is already in an unstable phase, then you should protect yourself against acute temptation through an antiflirt program. Always make it clear that you are in a solid relationship. Talk about your relationship and acknowledge it. Wear a wedding ring, and put up pictures of your partner and your children at work. Don't meet colleagues privately one-on-one. Avoid being alone with a person you're attracted to. Don't exchange phone numbers, and don't call back if that person calls you. Don't get into a car alone with that person. Don't return any "accidental" looks or touches. When in doubt, react as if your partner were physically present.

How to Fend off a Poacher. Prepare a couple of defense lines for yourself: "My wonderful husband would not like this at all; I'm going home to him now." "Thank you for the compliments. But that's enough. I prefer to put my energy into my own committed relationship." End a flirtation that's already underway with the sentence: "This was nice here with you. But we have to stop. Any more would put a strain on my relationship with my wife. And that relationship is my first priority."

What Can You Do After an Affair? If you want to rescue your relationship after an affair, we recommend proceeding according to the following behavioral-therapeutic concept. It comes from a therapy plan

for couples dealing with infidelity, that was developed by couples therapist Christoph Kröger at Braunschweig Polytechnic University. We know now that the betrayed partner experiences a trauma—a difficult, long-lasting wound. For this reason, the Braunschweig solution model uses elements from trauma therapy. The goal is to avoid further injury and to rebuild trust step-by-step. Infidelity doesn't have to mean the immediate end of the relationship, although it has massive consequences. The couple has one chance to win back their relationship: when they are able to turn the end of the affair into the beginning of healing their relationship.

1. *End the affair immediately and permanently.* The person who has been unfaithful must immediately separate from the extramarital relationship—clearly, convincingly, once and for all. Tell the third party that it's over and that you will never see each other again. Don't hesitate a single day. It's already been going on too long.

2. *Curb your accusations.* If you're in the position of the deceived party, you have suffered a severe blow and are traumatized. Don't let your pain eat you up inside. Find a counselor or therapist to help you as an impartial expert. Cry and express your rage over the betrayal. At the same time, during this tricky phase it also makes sense not to constantly throw accusations at your faithless partner. You are already deeply wounded, and every attack just makes it hurt more.

3. *Put up a stop sign against fighting.* Settle on a code word that you as a couple can use to stop each other when an argument threatens to escalate. Try to steer clear of misunderstandings so that the distance between you doesn't get bigger.

4. *Avoid further separations.* Many couples consider a temporary separation after an affair has taken place. But the research on infidelity has shown that this isn't wise. The affair already has a separating

effect, so you shouldn't increase it. Christoph Kröger recommends you find activities to do together instead—things that you are both good at. Concentrate on yourselves as a couple. Also, keep your friends out of it and don't discuss the situation with them. Most of them like to choose a side and can drive you further apart by poisoning the climate (e.g.,"You poor thing! How could she do that to you?" "After everything you've done for him, this is just unbelievable!").

5. *Clarify your positions.* Get to the bottom of the conflict. Come to an understanding of how to make sense of the situation before and after the affair. Only then can you gradually get closer to each other again. During your conversations, make sure that you both get a chance to speak. Trade off between listening and talking.

6. *Summarize your perspective.* Formulate your view of things in a letter to your partner. You should both ask yourselves: "What would it be like if we made a successful new beginning?" Move with heart and mind toward a new vision of your relationship. Write down as definitively as possible how your relationship realistically should be in the future. What would you like to do for it? What do you expect and hope for from your partner?

7. *Give yourself time.* Don't look at the affair as proof that your relationship is irretrievably shattered. Commit to a period of about a year. It takes many months to cope with the traumatic consequences of infidelity. During this time you should both decide if you want to stay together. Do a lot of good for yourselves during this time. Both partners have a chance to conquer the crisis when they are able to look forward and do something good for one another every day.

8. *Both take responsibility for the affair.* Though this sounds harsh to the betrayed partner at first, this is the best solution. The primary responsibility obviously lies with the person who has been unfaithful. But if you only see the evil criminal in the other person, you're left with the role of the victim. Victims have little freedom of action; they feel they are at someone else's mercy and can hardly help themselves. On the other hand, if you are ready to take on

your part of the responsibility and accept that things weren't optimal in your relationship before the affair, you can gain more power. Consider yourself on equal footing with your partner, and contribute your unmistakable part to the reconciliation.

9. *Reconcile.* From the view of the betrayed person, an affair is an unforgivable error. So it would be wrong to ask *forgiveness* for the betrayal and to expect that to make everything better. Asking for forgiveness makes the unfaithful person weak and passive, and the betrayed person strong and active—everything else depends on the betrayed person's mercy. This wouldn't be a relationship solution on equal footing. Instead, strive for a slow process of reconciliation. The unfaithful one should express his or her failure: "I did you an injustice and caused you pain. I regret it from the bottom of my heart. I want to make it up to you. I want to show you that I love you, and I'll do everything to make you happy with me so you can patch things up with me." This is how to take responsibility and show that one is capable of action. If you've been unfaithful, take advantage of this chance for reconciliation. Your great pain shows you that there is still a lot of love inside of you. If the reconciliation is successful on your side, let your partner know. Don't keep returning to the mistake. You can finally be finished with it.

10. *Trust the power of your heart.* This exercise is especially effective when both partners agree to it for two weeks. Sit together and draw the great heart of your relationship. In this heart, silently write all of the positive qualities and energies that you are missing right now in your relationship. If you want the same thing as your partner, circle the thought he or she has written down. Don't discuss or censor these points. Understand what you've written as your longings for something that is greater than you—as wishes on the heart that holds you both up, which can be fulfilled.

Each of you on your own should take this wish list in your hand every day and visualize these qualities pouring forth out of the great foundation of your relationship. Open your own heart as wide as possible. When you feel one of the desired qualities growing inside of you, don't resist it. Carry it quietly around with you. In the next two weeks, concentrate with curiosity on yourself and your partner. Trust that your couple's heart will daily send you exactly the qualities you wish for. Greet every little sign with gratitude and with a confident heart.

The Enemies of Love

You have love to thank for your life. Even if it was only a brief spark between your parents, this flash of love led to your conception. Then there was a longer-lasting glow of love with which you were raised, nourished, and protected until you became an adult. Songs are sung for this love; it is celebrated in poems, honored in religions, and held in our hearts.

But many people also have lost sight of the power of love. They received too little of it as children or have experienced a great disappointment. These people can't stand when others are successful with love. So they work against relationships, help people have affairs, make jokes about fidelity, and advise separation and divorce. Many do this unconsciously, others knowingly. Many are highly intelligent, others are just mimicking what they've heard elsewhere.

Don't Trust Every Piece of Advice. The enemies of love aren't easy to recognize. Some come to you in the form of your best friend or as relationship experts. What unites them all is a deep wound in their hearts. Under this wound, they are longing for exactly what you (still) have with your relationship. If you fail, like they have, it brings a little bit of comfort to them.

In many separations and divorces you often find ominous advisers. Sometimes it's a book, a film, or a conversation in which you're encouraged to no longer love, but rather to hate; to no longer trust, but to mistrust; to no longer build, but to destroy; to no longer listen, but to shout.

■ *Keep love at the table.* When you are in a conversation with a professional or private counselor, imagine that love is sitting there with you, perhaps in the form of an angel—that only you can see. How does the love angel respond to your counselor: does she stay at your counselor's side, or can you see  her turning away from that person? The counselor can deceive your reason with what he or she says. The purpose of the angel is to help you to rely on your intuition, which is much more intelligent in matters of the heart.

■ *Add even more chairs.* If your relationship is in a crisis, you will occasionally need to talk about your partner with a third person, while your partner isn't there. You should at least imagine your partner present as a listener. Would your partner feel good about this conversation? A key factor to getting good advice from an outside person is whether that person has a strong positive image of a "couple" in his or her heart. Can that person see you as a couple in crisis, or does that person just see two people who aren't getting along well and should separate?

■ *Hold on to your spiritual roots.* If you are anchored by religion, the enemies of love have a harder time influencing you. A sentence like "Love never stops," in the Song of Songs is always stronger than the bad experiences of other individuals.

Unemployment, Illness, Tough Times

In earlier times, more people settled in the kingdom of love. The homestead didn't stand as isolated as it does today in its fields; there were more lights and occupied cabins in the dark forest. People looked out for each other. Back then, couples were carried along by extended families, and outside problems were shouldered by many more people than they are today. Small families, which are a product of industrialization and bourgeois society, often endure unbelievable strains—and these families commonly collapse beneath it. Actually, the binding love between two people should help defend them from the attacks of natural forces and social hardships.

It is a pity how this relationship is slowly being turned on its head, as many relationships and marriages shatter under these outside influences, instead of being resilient. Because of stress at work, unemployment, debt, illness, and political and economic tensions, the relationship becomes the eye of the storm but then disintegrates. The time when a person needs love's help the most is when love is lost.

But this is not a law of nature. On the contrary, it should be the exact opposite. Remember the enormous power that lies in love, so you can defend yourself against external attacks.

Hold Each Other Tightly. Literally. When something bad happens (regardless of whose fault it was), quietly hug your partner. This is a bodily meditation, a technique that beyond all rational considerations, all accusations and self-accusations, all despair and sorrow, and all anger and helplessness is directly understood by you and your partner's soul as: "We will get through this," "We are strong together," or "This won't knock us down." Imagine that you are standing on

the great heart of your relationship. The sea is raging all around you, but together you are on safe ground.

Name the Common Enemy. In times of crisis, you are surrounded by a multitude of enemies, external as well as internal. Unfortunately, you always see the inner ones first: "You were being stupid, that's why you got fired," "I got so sick because you were never there for me," "You wasted our money," and so on. Instead of turning against each other, act like settlers during the Wild West: your top priority are the hordes of enemies who are attacking your little house. You have to fight them, and they are always easy to name. With debts it's a creditor, with unemployment it's an employer, and with sickness it's a virus or another cause. Together you can fight against these enemies with the weapons of your love. The enemy would prefer to have you separated so he or she could more easily conquer you. Don't do the enemy this favor. Stay together—be completely there for each other and stay close.

Envision Your Future Together. Love is not logical and not restrained. It can work miracles and make the impossible possible. In your mutual connection lies unimagined strength and possibilities. The great heart upon which you stand conceals buried treasure still waiting to be found. Invent a great future for yourself, conquering your enemies—regardless of how the circumstances around you may look. This is the energy and promise of love. This is what it was made for. This is the greatest thing you can experience.

Simplifying Idea 18: Go Your Separate Ways Respectfully

With a breakup or divorce, you must build a new life for yourself. This phase is especially difficult because you are so wounded. The following tips help you better orient yourself in this difficult situation and avoid typical mistakes.

Take Control of Your Divorce

Seek Advice from Other Divorced People. A typical mistake to isolate yourself in your disappointment. The consequence is that you miss out on important information others can offer. To get you ready for life without a partner, it's better to use the knowledge of as many single people who have had similar experiences of separation as you can. The others know how to cope with everyday life. Meet regularly

with a group of other divorced people, and get practical tips and moral support for your situation. Ask friends for help. Entrust yourself to a therapist. Get professional support from a good attorney who fights for you but who doesn't badger your partner.

Inform Your Employer and Your Colleagues. A typical mistake is to take your private problems with you to work and overwhelm everyone with them. The consequence is that you have no "other world" anymore: your crisis spreads to your work life. It's better to briefly inform your boss that you are going through a divorce. Don't get emotional, and don't try to make your boss your consoler or adviser. You will gain understanding and maintain your respect. Let your colleagues know about your difficult private situation, but protect your dignity and don't talk to them about confrontations or other intimate details. Thank your team for the support that they represent for you right now. Don't expect special treatment, and they will be more willing to make allowances for you on occasion.

Maintain Your Connection to Your Friends. A typical mistake is to try to get your shared circle of friends on your side by complaining about your ex-partner. The consequence is that in addition to having lost your partner, you also lose your friends. It's better to go to your mutual friends and tell them that you would like to continue being friends with them. Don't ask them to choose between you and your ex. The field will become clear on its own by and by. Bring old and new friends together.

Learn to Accept the Unavoidable. A typical mistake is that if you've been left and didn't want the separation or divorce, things are especially hard and you torture yourself with questions: "Why me? Why now? Why did he or she do this to me?" The consequence is that your freedom of action disappears. It's better to say stop to all self-doubts. Set yourself on "self-rescue." Concentrate on improvements, even tiny ones. Don't play the grump. Poisonous comments you make also poison you. Start an "I've done it on my own" bank, and enter your accomplishments there: ironed a shirt yourself, went to the movies by yourself, and rented a new apartment by yourself. Write down all the advantages of being alone, and try to add a new point to this list every day. This will help you develop new strengths and get a feeling for your own inner strength.

Keep an Eye on Your Attorney and Your Finances. A typical mistake is to leave everything to the attorney or ask the attorney to undertake a campaign of revenge to financially punish your ex-spouse. The consequence is that both methods severely limit your opportunity to form a good separation solution. A better idea is to not take the first lawyer who comes along. Find a serious attorney who can show you different paths for solving problems in your situation and their consequences. Work openly and honestly together with your attorney. Going behind your attorney's back, keeping something from your attorney, or lying to your attorney will only hurt you in the end. A divorce is also a business matter. For this you need a clear head and a sense of reality. Let go of unrealistic "maximum" demands. Go for the good-enough solution. Write down your ideas and wishes specifically and argue confidently to get what you need. In all your negotiations with your ex, ask to have it in writing.

Immediately make an objective and realistic list of priorities for your financial situation and stick to it. Set an absolute spending limit for yourself. Set aside a fixed amount at the beginning of every month.

Deal Rationally with Yourself and Your Ex. A typical mistake is to act on instinct and blindly follow your negative feelings. The consequence is that the wounds can't heal, and you stay bound by hostility to your ex. A better idea is to avoid revenge, and ignore spitefulness. Don't speak badly of your ex. Give yourself rules for dealing with your ex; otherwise he or she will take control. You now have a new role and should shape this new level of the relationship so that you can protect your autonomy and self-respect. Stop taking care of your ex or letting your ex take care of you. The more independently you live, the better you will get through the pain of separation. Your self-esteem will also grow. Stick to the agreements made during the divorce, especially with regard to the children. Hold on to your good memories of the time you had together.

Redefine the Parental Role. A typical mistake is that after the divorce, you think you can make all decisions concerning the children on your own. The consequence is that you create a new imbalance and provoke difficult confrontations, which are hard on your children. It's better to clearly distinguish between what you want and what is good for the children. A child cannot be divorced from his or her parents. Your ex remains father or mother to your children, even if you have full custody. Support the relationship between your ex and your children. Adhere to the arranged times for your children to see your ex. Make sure that the children are ready on time—your former spouse sees the children less often, so every minute is precious. Let them talk on the phone between visits. Send your ex photos of the children. Inform your ex about school matters, vacation plans, and career aspirations. Don't just let the holidays roll around. Make new concrete plans for birthdays, family celebrations, and Christmas. How should they be celebrated now? Make new traditions!

Keep Your Kids Grounded. A typical mistake is that you think your kids don't understand very much because they're still young or don't call attention to themselves. The consequence is that you overlook warning signs. Today, divorce is the greatest threatening factor in the life of a child, not illness or accidents. Don't leave your children to deal with it alone! It's better to keep teachers and caretakers informed about the situation. Children often unconsciously feel guilty for their parents' divorce, and so they react desperately. Their schoolwork can also suffer. Talk to teachers and the school counselor about what help your child can receive in this difficult situation. In addition, make sure your child has at least one solid, reliable adult figure whom he or she can turn to besides Mom and Dad. Studies show that this decreases the stress associated with divorce for children. Don't use your child as a substitute for your partner. Don't lie to your children, and don't entrust them with intimate details about the relationship. Even if you've been hurt badly, you should never disparage your partner in front of the children! Your children will feel an inner solidarity with the other parent, even if it's only unconsciously. Don't gripe about the parenting style of your ex. Instead, try to come to an agreement with your ex on important child-rearing goals, for the purpose of giving your child more clarity. Come up with set rules that apply to both parents.

Support Relationships with Relatives. A typical mistake is to not want to have anything to do with the "other" relatives and break off all contact with them. The consequence is your children are cut off from their background. It's better to realize that while your relationship may be over, your children are still related to your ex's family. Ask your former parents-in-law how they imagine the future family relations. Make an open offer to maintain friendly relations. Support your children by staying in contact with the other grandparents. Invite them together with your ex to important occasions (e.g., communion, school events, the children's weddings).

Simplifying Idea 19: Re-Create Your Relationship

When you seriously consider ending your relationship, you reach the darkest corner of the dark forest, the place of total disorientation for yourself and hopelessness for the couple. You are in a state of conflict with yourself or with your partner, you could doubt yourself or your partner, you are furious and sad, and you feel guilty or lost, persecuted or left alone.

The normal reaction would be to run away from this darkest point or to shut your eyes. But if you do this, love becomes blinded and dies.

One of love's many secrets is that it is precisely in this darkest point that it wants to open your eyes and lead you to the one place on your love map where you can find your way out of the darkness.

The Settlement: Help in the Dark Forest

Trust love one last time before you give up altogether. Take one last risk. In the darkness, open the eyes of your heart—eyes that can see  further than your understanding can. These eyes don't see what's lost, but what's still to come, what's waiting for you as a couple beyond the chaos.

Grasp the Lifeline. In the dark forest there is more than just the crooked witch houses and eerie robbers' caves, the noise of the dragon fights, the rattling chains of the horsemen of the apocalypse, and the nightmare of separation. In the middle of this darkness of your loneliness and desperation is also a rescuing lifeline, a peaceful space. We call this the settlement. One of the greatest insights of psychology is that every person has this inner place of refuge in his or her soul. You find this place in myths about the Holy Grail as well as in mystical traditions.

Your Greatest Helper: Your Imagination. Imagine this modest settlement in as much detail as possible. If you were to paint a picture, how would this hideaway and the space around it look? Which plants would grow there? Settlers like to build their shelters near a spring so they can have fresh water—can you see this spring? When you have become familiar with this place, take heart and call to the settler who lives here. Calmly observe his appearance. What does he look like? What is he wearing? If you sense love and trust, go toward him in your mind.

Entrust Yourself to Your Good Settler. The good settler is the symbol of an inner, hidden strength of your soul that can come to your rescue. Despite his remoteness, your inner settler sits along the well of knowledge. He has access to the waters of the unconscious and can lead you inward from the outside. He can appear in your dreams or through your consciousness, calling on your inner vision. Usually he speaks to you in a kind of old-fashioned archaic language. You recognize him by his understanding, calm, comforting, and reconciliatory way of speaking. He can appear to you in the form of a wise man or woman. When you are near this figure, you feel security and affirmation. You can ask for advice. Face your inner settler as realistically as possible. Approach him with open arms. Seek his guidance, and ask him to help you.

Answer the Disentanglement Questions. The confusion of feelings within you has made you irrational. The presence of your inner settler helps you summarize your problem briefly and soberly, perhaps through the following kinds of questions:

- What have I not yet understood? What should I be open to?
- What is now the most important thing in my difficult situation?
- Where are my inner barriers? And those of my partner?
- What is the rescuing strength now?
- What is the hidden meaning of my life?

Imagine that the settler asks you quietly: "What do you want to achieve, in the bottom of your loving heart? What good should come out of it in the end?" Listen inside of you; think of the future and answer this question calmly. Afterward, ask him to show you the first three good steps in that direction. This will help you avoid overhasty, reactive solutions.

Choose the Path of Greatest Resistance. Your wise inner settler is the symbolic figure of letting go for the sake of love. He has devoted himself to this basic need of your soul. He won't be contented with small repairs; he wants something great to come out of you as a person, as well as out of you and your partner as a couple. For this he has learned to walk the path of greatest resistance. This is the only way he can master the two powerful drives that are responsible for many people's conflicts: the drive for unlimited power over others and

for unlimited sexual satisfaction. The drive for power puts the other partner under pressure, controls him or her through money, and presses hard on the partner through physical or emotional superiority. The sex drive demands either a forcible acting out or suppression of lust; it makes you into the betrayer or the one who refuses, and your partner into the betrayed or the one who is denied. In both cases, there is no longer a loving I and no longer a loving We.

Gain by Going Without in the Right Way. Your inner settler is your best support for overcoming this crisis of the missing I and We. Let yourself be patiently led by him. Have no fear; he will not advise you to give up sex forever or to let go of your inner authority. He will neither force you nor rush you. Rather, he will help you find your personal way to learn to stop blindly acting out both drives, for your own and your relationship's sake. If you follow his wisdom, you will feel an essential fundamental change to take place inside of you.

Flow Inward. Here is an extra simplifying suggestion for men: Many women find their inner hermit in the middle of life. They turn inward because they sense that it brings them closer to their souls. They also long for intellectual exchange about their inner processes. They often complain of being left alone in this. Their husbands don't want to have any of their own authentic experiences with their souls (e.g., "If it does something for you, fine—but it's not my kind of thing."). Talk to your partner about whether she feels a similar longing. Ask her to tell you, if she wants, about her inner images. Listen to her, and at the same time listen inside yourself. As soon as something touches you inside, give your partner a sign that it resonates with you: "I know that feeling too." Allow your soul to flow over into the emotional world of your partner. This does good for your partner as well as helps you develop a feeling for your own inner journey—which will feel very different, probably somewhat rawer and wilder.

With Your Hand over Your Heart: Feel the Couple's Heart Beating.
After the cleansing of the settlement, your deepest being follows one wonderful piece of wisdom, the desire to entrust itself to love from now on despite all questions in the relationship. Imagine that you are kneeling down on the great floating heart and you lay your hand on its surface.

Feel how this heart beats from deep within—gentle, calm, but powerful beats. With your hand still on the great heart underneath you, say: "I'm staying here." Tell the heart what has happened up until now: how you have been hurt, how your partner is perhaps still obstinate, how you still can't open yourself to the other person, and yes, even how at the moment you don't even want to see the other person. In spite of all this, you open yourself to the great couple's heart and hear it beating and pumping.

Let Energy Flow into You. Looking at the heart of your relationship, say: "Fill me up again." When you say this sentence, you open yourself up for the greatest power on earth. This power is just waiting to rejuvenate your relationship. In the next section you will learn how you can help this power along.

Discover Your Evolution as a Couple

At this present point, you will find the key to the happy future of your relationship not in cool analysis or rational planning, but rather in the discovery of a new vision as a couple. We're talking about a special kind of vision; at the same time, it is old and new, small and large, *evolutionary* and *revolutionary*.

The Revolution of Your Relationship. Your evolution as a couple is something completely new. You work toward a new goal and are on the verge of making a brand-new bond for life with your old partner (whom you're now experiencing in new ways).

- *The healing chaos.* The evolution of a couple as a revolt against old patterns usually begins with one of you. The revolt is supported by the heart that you share as a couple. The rejuvenating energy wells up from there and wants to grab both of you. This revolution is no mere maneuver of your partner's, but rather an absolutely necessary step toward the healing transformation of your relationship. It dissolves set patterns and conventional power relations in your relationship. At first, it causes confusion. This phase of disorientation also makes way for something new, though. This is the chance for both of you to find a new order that is greater than your previous ideas of relationship.

- *Find the greater togetherness.* After a revolution, a state needs a group of its smartest minds to formulate a new constitution. In the same way, your partnership needs a new basic law that you both are subject to from now on. This new constitution is love. This is the future that the relationship revolution opens up to you; you submit yourself to love, not to your partner.

Good energy flows out of the couple's heart, independent of your behavior and that of your partner. Through this power, you both become lovers once again. You experience a love that is greater than you and your partner. It flows warmly through both of you and takes hold of your souls.

The Evolution of Your Heart. Your evolution as a couple is a revolutionary change and at the same time a dynamic push toward evolution. It builds upon what the two of you have created together. Over the course of your relationship, you have developed towards each other and adapted yourselves to each other. In the end, even if you don't want to be together any more or you are suffering from the sacrifices you made for the relationship, your unity, the shared heart beneath you, is a fact. And you can trust it.

- *Look at it "Hawaiian-style.* "In Polynesian, this unity is called *Lokahi*. In the old Hawaiian culture, there were no divorces. Such an intense relationship between two people who love each other, they were convinced, couldn't be broken. The partners could live apart and start new relationships, but they didn't buy into the illusion that *Lokahi* could erase the first relationship. This spared them a lot of anger and hate, because the many negative emotions that arise during the separation process are, above all, related to the foolish desire to erase the past.

- *Celebrate your progress.* Through your experiences in the dark forest, you both have changed. You've been pushed to your limits and have learned new abilities. Your partner, whom you wanted to send off to the moon not too long ago, is no longer the same. And you, too, have powerfully transformed.

How to Find Your New Vision. Back when you were lying in the love tent, the air in the tent was swimming with visions that both of you dreamed for yourselves as a couple. The love tent owes its appeal to the thoughts of the future that stream into the lives of the two lovers when they dream new dreams for their relationship. With the help of your inner visions, which you both poured into your relationship back then, your shared life emerged. There were spoken and unspoken goals, such as "We want to be a family with our own home," "We want to enjoy life and go on wonderful journeys together," "We want to take over Dad's company and throw ourselves into this work," "We want to someday go to Africa and work in a clinic," or "We want to get involved in our community."

Now you need a new vision—an image, an idea that is worth striving for. The magnitude of this vision determines the magnitude of your relationship. This vision as a couple is not the idea of one of the two partners, but rather it's an image that is hidden in the treasure of your floating couple's heart. Here's how to coax your visions into the light.

- *Renew the pact.* Make your partner into your ally. Often, the other person has a clearer vision for your dreams and wishes than you do yourself. Make a pact with each other about finding a new vision for the two of you. Give each other the task of finding out which current concerns and ideas of the future each of you has.

- *Bring out recurring images.* Start by looking back over important stations in your history together. Talk over your variations on these stories. Remember your visions from back in the love tent. Look for the images that used to guide you. Which ones are now used up, and which are still glimmering and can be reignited?

- *Write with both hands.* Imagine that you are your partner. Sit in your partner's usual spot in your home. Write on a blank sheet of paper: "This is how I want to live." Then take the pen in your other hand (i.e., the hand you usually don't write with), and write down what answers occur to you (i.e., as your partner). You will be surprised. While the rational side of your brain is completely absorbed with the tricky job of writing with the wrong hand, hidden aspects of your inner self often come out; the visions of your partner appear before your eyes in those shaky letters.

- *Let go of old plans.* To come into a new vision, you have to let go of the old one. Perhaps one of you had the idea: "We want to build our own home for the family." If the children have already moved out, this idea can change: "Maintaining a house costs too much money, energy, and time. We can sell it; we'll move into an apartment and have more resources for what's important to us now." The old picture of "buy a house" wasn't wrong. But now it is time to replace it. You recognize a renewed vision of your relationship by the way that it addresses both partners, motivates them, and fills them with joy once more. It convinces both of you that you will gain more than you will lose.

- *Search out good role models.* Look for other couples in your surroundings, both younger and older. Who would you like to learn something from? Where do you both say: "This couple does something well, let's do it that way, too." Don't be afraid to ask the couple explicitly for advice: "We like the way you talk to each other, your lifestyle, your division of labor, your relaxed attitude toward money . . . how do you do that?"

- *Journey into the future.* If you're a more imaginative type, try the time-traveling method. Sit down, relax, close your eyes, and imagine an actual date in the future: Christmas 2020, your seventieth birthday, your oldest daughter's wedding. Keeping your eyes closed, describe your surroundings as exactly as possible and including even the boring details: Where are you? Where is your partner? What are you wearing? How is the weather? What are you concerned with at the moment? Who is with you? Make an effort not to imagine or make anything up, rather just observe. Don't worry if you can't conjure any images! Your vision may still be hiding, but you have already begun to call it forth with this exercise. It will show itself perhaps in the next few days—all of a sudden, for example, as you're brushing your teeth or folding laundry.

- *Talk to your future self.* Another proven exercise is this variant of the journey through time: your future self visits you. Imagine sitting across from yourself, a wise, clever person, who is ten or twenty years older than you. Ask what you as a couple, in your future self's opinion, are doing wrong at the moment and what vision is worthwhile for the two of you. Or have your future self write you a letter with suggestions. Your true self, that clever being outside of time, has heard the questions and will answer them.

- *Collect images.* If you were a painter or sculptor, how would you represent your vision as a couple? Sometimes a symbol

187

will crystallize, such as a great old tree that you sit under together or a raft that brings you over a sea. Sometimes it's also a story, a fairy tale, a song, or a film that symbolizes your vision for you. Find and collect images, photos, videos, and copies of it. Are there some that you both click with? Use such images as a background on your computer, put one up in your home, or carry one in your wallet.

- *Rewrite your screenplay.* Develop scenarios with multiple variations. Imagine that you're writing a screenplay with alternative suggestions for a strange couple struggling with the same problem. Perhaps you've seen the film Groundhog Day, in which a cynical reporter slowly transforms into a person capable of love by living through countless variations of the same day. There are just as many chances in the two of you for things to go well!

- *Shake the apple tree.* Being struck by your couple's vision is different from finding goals that are hiding somewhere. The great couple's vision doesn't feel like something falling on your head, but like a powerful image emerging from deep regions. Sometimes it is physically perceptible directly from the heart and stays in your memory for a long time, like emotionally meaningful dreams. As soon as you have discovered a component of your vision, it will give you energy for moving toward that vision. This is like shaking a fruit tree; your effort is necessary to reach the fruit. But the fruit itself doesn't come from you.

Stay Grounded. Don't be intimidated by the grandness of your fairy tale vision. Expand your possibilities in small steps. Experiment with new variations in your everyday life. Every morning, discuss what you both can do differently and better today than before, and how you can connect your insights to those of your partner. Often, it takes three weeks to change a habit. Don't give up too easily; check your progress in six weeks, at the earliest.

So step-by-step, you come closer to the goal, leaving the dark forest. The next, the fifth and last, station in the landscape of love is our symbol for the fairy tale vision that you are nearing on your way through the land of love: your new dwelling, the castle.

The Fifth Dwelling of Love
The Castle

Your Simplifying Dream: The Castle

You wake up because you hear some cheerful sounds. You can hear dance music playing somewhere below, along with the typical sounds of a celebration: glasses clinking, people talking and laughing together, footsteps on a pebbled walk. As you open your eyes, you look at a large balcony door standing open, through which a gentle light shines on you. It's a warm summer evening; the sun is just setting and casting its warm glow into your room. You are lying in a great bed, and now you get up curiously and go to the window. What you see makes you catch your breath and your heart skip. From the curved balustrade you look out onto a sensational panorama; on the horizon is the fiery sliver of sun, and before it lay gentle wooded hills as far as the eye can see. Closer lie green and yellow fields with farmhouses, some with their windows already lit up. To your right, your eyes are drawn up to a mighty tower and a second one next to it, both joined by a boldly swinging bridge, which hangs many feet above you over a great courtyard. There, many stories below you, a party is in full swing. The music, which you now hear more clearly, comes from a small orchestra that is playing on a candlelit pavilion. In the middle of a courtyard, a tall fountain bubbles.

You hear the door to your room open and a very familiar voice says, "Darling, everyone is waiting for us!" Your beloved comes to you on the balcony and puts an arm around you. At this moment, the music stops. The people in the courtyard stop and look up at you on the balcony.

> They begin to applaud, some calling out. The person next to you holds you tighter, and suddenly everything is clear. "How magnificent," you say, "they're celebrating us. Let's go down to them."

Do you remember your tower and the needs of your soul? Souls can grow to be quite enormous and fill up enormous inner rooms. This is also true for your shared soul, this great floating heart that carries both of you together. During the time in the homestead, it has grown and you've gained a new depth of self. You have suffered and overcome difficulties in the dark forest. This has made your shared soul even stronger. This is all well and good—but what now?

Start at a New Place

Now something special, something wonderful begins. At the end of your journey through the kingdom of love, you move into your castle. When we talk about this in our lectures or seminars, many in the audience listen with tears in their eyes. Some of them are overcome by the prospect of a phase of enjoyment following all of the stresses and strains of living together—an idea that is missing from the counsel of most relationship advisers. Others realize that they have already arrived in the castle, "We've sensed this for a long time, but this is the first time we've heard it put into words."

You have the love that has grown between you to thank for your castle. Your love built it for you. The castle is a gift through and through, even if the path that brought you here has taken great effort on both your parts. The love that you experience in the castle as the royal couple is the same love that you knew in the love tent, that held you together in the homestead, and which you desperately sought in the dark forest. At the same time, the love in the castle is new. It is greater, but quieter; superior, but more modest. It is a celebration of enjoying each other and is at the same time filled with a mysterious stillness.

Take a Tour of Your Castle

On this tour, you will encounter the spaces of your previous experiences as you have integrated them into your castle. Together, they now form a new meaningful entity.

The Castle's Mountain. The castle lies above a settlement at the base of a mountain rising out of the dark forest. C. G. Jung linked this mountain to "the great towering of the adult personality." The strenuous climb up the mountain symbolizes the "struggle of becoming conscious," which you have bravely faced.

> **Simplifying Tip:** Adopt a new ritual. When you've overcome a stressful phase in your relationship, have a "celebration for two heroes." The difficult stage has been surmounted, the struggle has paid off, and you can congratulate yourselves. ■

The Drawbridge. This represents your new ability to better protect your relationship against stressful influences. Together you can decide when you want to have the gate open. As the royal couple, threats from the dark forest no longer throw you off course. You can react more calmly and with more flexibility should your partner stray there again. The dark forest remains dark, but the castle gives you support and security.

> **Simplifying Tip:** Agree on a small signal that you can use to quietly communicate your need for emotional support when in the company of others. As the royal pair, you can

now pull away together at any time and keep yourselves out of the problems of your adult children or other relatives. You can take time for just the two of you—time when you're not available for anyone else. ■

The Towers. Since the time the two of you "tied the knot," your individual towers have grown even taller and have gained beautiful new crests as a symbol of your healthy seclusion. Many parts of your soul only matured fully once you were in this relationship. Now the towers are visible from miles away and bear the starred banner of love. They rise high into the sky, as a sign of the vast perspective that you have gained over the course of your relationship. You not only survey your own kingdom, but also have gained an awareness of the social and political arenas. The small towers stand for your children and your children's children, biological as well as spiritual.

> **Simplifying Tip:** As a couple, you have managed to transform your relationship on the way to the castle into an "adaptable system." As a citizen, demand this of your state and your society, which may perhaps try to hinder the unity of career and family. Don't wait for "someone else" to do something. Take action yourself! ■

The Love Tent. Sometimes, as quickly as it collapsed, the tent's light construction proved to be an advantage in the end. Your love tent could be broken down in its old place and reerected in a beautiful new spot in the castle garden. You don't need to wander into strange realms to encounter the magic of love. The tender or passionate love will be available to you as a royal couple with unexpected intensity.

> **Simplifying Tip:** Don't let your passion be determined by old patterns and frustrations. Start from the beginning. Relax yourself physically, without wanting to do or have anything. Your

loving hearts have the power to open up your bodies for each other again. ▪

The Economy Buildings. They are similar to your timber-framed homestead and stand for your shared lifework as a couple, as career people,  as parents, and as volunteers. In the castle you can see that you've always been building on something that is greater than the two of you alone. So your view shifts more and more from having to being, from the material to the personal.

> **Simplifying Tip:** As a royal couple, you have not only the right but indeed the obligation to support other people with your positive experiences. Find networks in which you can offer your life experience and abilities (e.g., associations, Internet forums, churches, self-help groups). This way, you contribute to the well-being of society. ▪

The Hall of Ancestors. This gallery lies in the center of your castle and symbolizes the reconciliation of both of your extended families and previous partners. No one is excluded here, everyone is honored, and each has his or her place. There are no family ghosts to work their mischief in your castle.

> **Simplifying Tip:** Even when real reconciliation is impossible because the person concerned has broken contact with you or has even passed away, you can still accomplish this internally. Whatever has happened, no one can ask of your soul that you return evil for evil. Allow your loving soul to look upon everyone with friendliness, reconciliation, and sovereignty in the best sense. ▪

The Diplomats' Chamber. Here there are empty suits of armor standing next to the doors, and the weapons of old hang peacefully on the wall. As royalty, you no longer fight like you once did, but deal more diplomatically with the decisions of the majority. You are more reliable, calmer, more ready to compromise, and better at anticipating the needs of the other person.

> **Simplifying Tip:** Tell your partner when you feel positively supported and appreciated by him or her. A good diplomat never skimps on praise and admiration, but wraps his or her critique in positive feedback—diplomatically. People accept occasional criticism better when they've recently been praised. ■

The Throne Room. In the castle you have space to celebrate life and enjoy each other.

> **Simplifying Tip:** Constantly renew the legend of your relationship. Celebrate anniversaries in your relationship (e.g., when you first met, your engagement, your wedding). Tell your children about these times, and look at your old photos. Have yourselves photographed together as often as possible. Celebrate your most original personal moments together: the day he dug the wrong car out of the snow, or the day that you both lost your keys. Enter these kinds of moments into a calendar, and make up small rituals that are fitting to each event. ■

The Chapel. This is a symbol of your spiritual awareness that all of your success wasn't brought on by your actions, but rather was a gift.

> **Simplifying Tip:** Imagine that an uplifting saying that you both like to read hangs on the wall in your chapel, "I bless you, and you shall be a blessing." Speak this blessing inwardly to your

partner. Bless everything that your partner comes in contact with. This strengthens your relationship, keeps your heart open, and also protects your children. ■

Simplifying Idea 20: Grasp the Big Picture

As a royal couple in the castle, you are like a common organism that works on its growth and in doing so considers many things, checks them over, accepts them, or tosses them away. You gain a sense for the big picture, and look over the broad panorama of your world and reality in general. As a "panorama couple," you can react to changing situations with more flexibility, calm, and strength than ever before.

Eight Words of Wisdom from Great Thinkers for Panorama Couples to Live By

Solidarity. As a panorama couple you will find that you can no longer distinguish between *mine* and *yours*. You have melted together over the great heart of your relationship, and you experience this as unity. The words of the Persian poet Rumi apply to you: "Never, in truth, does the lover seek without being sought by his beloved. When the light of love comes down into this heart, one must know that it also comes down into that heart. No clap sounds from one hand alone."

Caution. As a panorama couple, you encounter each other gingerly and cautiously. You dedicate yourselves to the inner state of your relationship with growing care. This way, you protect your love from injury and the other from damage. Follow the model of poet and filmmaker Jean Cocteau: "Each night I lie down happily if I have done nothing to hurt the person closest to me."

Devotion. As a panorama couple, you know in the depth of your heart that it is your most beautiful hope and your greatest wish to support and love each other with all tenderness and strength. Following this wisdom means not only conquering the other with the help of love but also yourself. What you experience as mature love for one another has been described by existential psychotherapist Uwe Böschemeyer thus: "It is as if the one has loved the other into being."

Richness. As a panorama couple, you're not interested in what the relationship can do for you. Or how the other can help you. Or whether it's worth it to stay together. Or whether it would be better, nicer, or easier with another partner. Don't make any more cost-benefit calculations. Your participation in the other isn't limited to just doing your part. As the Cistercian Balduin von Ford has said: "With the love that is in us two things are inseparably bound: the love of what we have together and the togetherness in love. If one of these is missing, then the love is not yet happy."

Loneliness. As a panorama couple, you have realized that each of you possesses an unfathomable fundamental being. The better you know each other, the greater your awareness of your own tower-uniqueness, which is for you alone and will always remain strange to the other. Like poet Rainer Maria Rilke, you know that a great love doesn't only consist of togetherness: "A good marriage is that in which each appoints the other guardian of his solitude, and shows him this confidence, the greatest in his powers to bestow." Think of love as a space in which two lonely people protect each other and each can "see the other whole and against a wide sky."

Comfort. As a panorama couple, it is obvious to you that you comfort and encourage each other. You live according to the words of the poet Paul Verlaine: "Nothing is better for the soul than to free the soul of another from sadness!" You are aware of the inner suffering of your partner and accompany him with understanding and empathy. Despite this, brooding and melancholy have no chance with you. You help each other against sadness with the clarity and cheerfulness that flows from your loving heart.

Simplicity. As a panorama couple, you grasp the complex reality of your relationship. But you don't allow your relationship to become complicated. Together you have found a perspective that makes you independent from the chaos in the realm of collective opinion. Over the years, you have shown the following sentence from Friedrich Schiller to be true: "Simplicity comes from maturity." Your love has reached a point of great minimalism because you both have found the point where you are completely at peace in your relationship.

Belief. As a panorama couple, you can discuss questions of belief. Explore the reaches of your faith through conversation. Tell each other your dreams. Share "sublime moments." Talk freely about your religious experiences, without holding back. Find common rituals of

faith that you both like and which do you good. Let go of images of faith that you have moved beyond, and motivate each other to explore anew the landscape of the soul. As expressed by Friedrich Schleiermacher, a spiritually sustainable relationship allows your soul to "become a soul within another."

Your I-You-We Path Through the Land of Love

Even though no road was laid out for you in the land of love, you can in retrospect trace the unmistakable path that has brought you to your castle. Looking back, you will see that the path wasn't coincidental; rather, it followed the mysterious swinging of a pendulum. The progression of the five dwellings of love created an invisible pattern that always brought your two drifting poles of I and We back together. The I represents the pole of autonomy; the We stands for the couple. The step in between is made by love through the friendly You, who hurries like a winged messenger back and forth between the two of you and invites you to adjust your course.

In the castle you both regain yourselves as transformed and more mature. I and You have become more true because they allow their souls to lead them. This makes a new encounter possible, thus renewing the We. The "being in a couple" and the "being oneself" are reconciled. Now you understand how to let the pendulum swing back and forth between I and We. At the same time, you pay careful attention to the You, which helps you keep in mind the balance between the poles.

Spiral Dynamics Integral—the Broad Overview

The I-You-We path is the path of you both together. But you two don't live alone in this world. With you are a million others on their own adventures through the kingdom of love. Each person experiences the journey as something entirely personal, and yet we are all influenced by the others. Viewed from a great distance, the consciousness process of all these millions of families, couples, and individuals forms a pattern.

This phenomenon is similar to a giant school of fish: each individual fish guides itself, but viewed altogether, the school has its own intelligence, which goes beyond each individual. The school avoids danger, has certain preferences, and seeks the most nourishing waters.

There is a similar group-intelligence at work with people. It's especially interesting to investigate the development of this collective consciousness over the centuries. Psychologists and consciousness researchers Clare Graves, Don Beck, and Christopher C. Cowan have been doing this for forty years and have summarized the results of countless worldwide development studies into one comprehensive system. They describe how human consciousness always comes up with new ideas of the world and thereby further develops itself. The swarm of humanity, according to their clear results, is becoming continuously more intelligent. Because this capability is to be seen in the most diverse cultures, the researchers speak of a general human principle.

Each form of human life, from the bushman to the global player, creates its own perception and interpretation of the world. This helps people to react to new challenges and to solve problems that arise,

because we can change our horizon and our self-organization when they become too narrow. We humans shift our focus to the next field, which makes more complex solutions possible. This also goes for couples and their development because they are part of the great swarm of humanity. A couple, consisting of two people, is the smallest form of a society. For that reason, we believe that the couple reacts especially sensitively to social changes.

Explore Your Psychological DNA. The collective intelligence of humans has so far developed in eight clearly distinguishable stages. Beck, Graves, and Cowan call them "memes." The concept of meme (pronounced "meem") comes from the Greek word *mneme*, meaning "memory." We'll stick with these terms to avoid confusion.

In one meme you find all of the biological survival rules, religious myths, philosophical convictions, ethical values, psychological knowledge, cultural practices, attitudes, and forms of community that are at this level of consciousness necessary for dealing with reality. Imagine the memes as living strands that flow into each other, and not as a hierarchical tier. Similar to the way that DNA contains the inheritance of millions of years of development in each cell, each meme contains the social, emotional, and religious development of all other memes. This is why the memes are also referred to as "psychological DNA." The memes also exist in both of you, and a part of the larger process of social change also takes place in your relationship.

The Secret of the Eight Colors. Beck, Graves, and Cowan use the image of a great upward-winding spiral for the development of the memes—and similarities to the curving structure of DNA are certainly no accident. New turns in this spiral have been developing as long as human consciousness has existed—around a hundred thousand years. At the beginning, this went very slowly, but by our present time it has come to move quite quickly. Each person goes through the entire spiral during development from infancy to adulthood. During this process, the memes are always gone through in the same order; the same levels of existence also appear in organizations, groups, societies, entire cultures—or in relationships.

So far, eight memes have been identified and described. A ninth meme is now dawning on the horizon of humanity. What comes after is uncertain, because the spiral is open at the top and symbolizes our unending striving upward.

For simplicity's sake, the memes are assigned colors and are divided into two groups. The first group is called the "First Tier." It covers the first six memes—Beige, Purple, Red, Blue, Orange, and Green—and is concerned with maintaining existence. In the Second Tier—with Yellow, Turquoise, and the tender beginnings of Coral—the best aspects of all the memes from the First Tier are used in the development of an information-oriented, mobile, and global society.

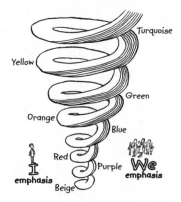

Memes Swing from I to We and Back Again. Interestingly, the memes regularly alternate in their emphasis on individual and community. In one meme, the I/Me/Mine gets its chance and strengthens the individual. As a countermovement, in the next meme the relationship comes into the foreground and emphasizes the We/Us/Our experience. Then in the next meme it's again about I/Me/Mine. This is often misunderstood as "now it goes back again," and many social processes are thought of as "reform," doing things like we did before. In reality, the pendulum actually swung from a We-era to an I-era, but on a higher level.

By now this is familiar to you from the five dwellings of love and your I-You-We path: in your relationship, you also swing back and forth between your individual needs and those of the couple. This is not a mistake; rather, it is part of the dynamic of the human consciousness.

The First Tier: The First Six Memes

1. *Beige: instinctive survival.* This first concept of human consciousness emerged around a hundred thousand years ago. You encoun-

ter it still today when you confront the basic survival of the individual. You feel it during times of mortal danger, illness, depression, and suicidal feelings. The more extreme living conditions become, the more Beige comes into play: in homelessness, for African AIDS victims, for the victims of traumatizing natural disasters, in concentration camps and genocides. You also find it in helpless newborns. Food, water, warmth, and security have the top priority. *Dualism:* there is only survival or death; I want to survive. *Emphasis:* I.

2. *Purple: magic and animism.* This meme emerged around fifty thousand years ago, when people bonded together to ensure their survival. They formed clans, tribes, families, and couples. Today, they have found associations, teams, and self-help groups. Sacred feasts, tribal rituals, yearly cycles, and personal rites of passage (e.g., marriage, testing, burial) are celebrated as group experiences. Purple takes care of the emotional glue in relationships. Exclusion from the group or family is the greatest threat that one must protect oneself against here. One is obedient to chiefs, elders, and the clan. The world takes on magical characteristics. It is teeming with good and evil creatures who bring blessings or curses. Film

epics like *The Lord of the Rings* or bestsellers like the Harry Potter series show that this world is still living within us and represents a protection against cool rationality. Children's stuffed animals, adults' amulets, and good luck charms—these are Purple, as are horoscopes and tarot cards. Lovers also watch over small objects belonging to their partner like treasures. Holy symbols, reliquaries, and sacraments also serve as protection for the relationship. *Dualism:* There are good ghosts and bad ghosts; I align myself with the good ones. *Emphasis:* We.

3. *Red: impulsive egocentrism.* Around ten thousand years ago, individuals began to detach themselves from their magical embedment in groups and families. Creative heroes set out bravely to free themselves from frozen traditions and to conquer new lands, "Be yourself and do what you want, disregard everything else." Pride, self-confidence, strength of individuality developed—an important and often misunderstood phase in the development of humanity and of each individual. Red helps defend against seduction, dependence, and oppression. Children go through this during the "terrible twos" and later again during puberty. Humiliation and critique are dangerous during this stage; there is a great need for respect. A weak I is easily ashamed, is overwhelmed by his or her emotions, and strikes out impulsively around him or her. When threatened, Red turns to physical violence or treachery. The Mafia is a Red organization, as are all terrorist groups in the world. People in love experience the tremendous power of Red eroticism in the love tent; they encourage each other and show great self-confidence. *Dualism:* There are the strong and the weak. I am one of the strong, regardless of what happens. *Emphasis:* I.

4. *Blue: goal-oriented authority.* As a balance to Red, Blue sets boundaries. Around five thousand years ago the first state and justice systems emerged. Rules and laws were defined: "Life had a meaning and a predetermined exit." Red was followed by order, infrastructure, norms, values, and virtues. The Blue system makes judgments about right and wrong and imposes punishments. Kingdoms and empires arise with moral conceptions and meaningful traditions. The power of impulsivity is controlled by a sense of guilt and obedience. In the relationship, Blue relies on virtues such as loyalty, diligence, punctuality, and politeness; you may often have a guilty conscience or blame something on your partner. The bonding We-feeling is especially strong in Blue.

Even the great world religions came about during this meme and bind the individual to the absolute whole. There is a redeeming beyond, which rewards the morally good with eternal life. *Dualism:* I am on the side of the holy; the others are sinners. *Emphasis:* We.

5. *Orange: strategic success.* After focusing on the world beyond, humanity began, around three hundred years ago, to examine the immediate world. The natural sciences boomed; modern states and industries arose. We started using the resources of the earth more intensively than ever before to create a life of abundance. Everyone is the master of his own happiness, and the Orange motto is, "Act in your own interest and play to win." God is out, and science is concerned with explaining the world. It investigates, measures, analyses, and differentiates. Even love is described as a genetic program of managing the drives. Sexual attraction becomes the measure of the relationship and is under pressure to perform. Men emphasize their rationality as opposed to the apparently deeper

emotionality of the woman. Relationship wars are fought over money. Thanks to increasing education, the couple begins to critically reflect upon their relationship. Optimistic researchers who study couples develop strategies for ever-improving partnerships on the basis of scientific studies. *Dualism:* There are winners and losers; I am a winner. *Emphasis:* I.

6. *Green: community and equality for all.* Around 150 years ago, the countermovement against the enormously successful Orange meme began. Green replaces materialism and achievement with empathy and humanity. The earth can no longer be exploited. Before, the external was studied; now the internal is explored. We seek peace inside of us and renew our own spirituality together with others. Willingness for dialogue and social responsibility provide us with the warmth that makes up a harmonious, loving

community. All people are equal; human rights are formulated. Decisions must be based on consensus, which can lead to weak leadership and stalemates caused by unending discussion. Minorities and the disadvantaged are valued and integrated. Man and woman have equal rights; power structures in marriage are  condemned. Each couple should subjectively decide what he and she like in the relationship, which calls for a narcissistic attitude. In cases of conflict, you threaten your partner with denial of love and show him or her your own injuries. If your partner does not fulfill your expectations anymore, the relationship is broken off. *Dualism:* Sensitive, aware people must always deal with unaware, insensitive people. *Emphasis:* We.

The Second Tier: The Next Memes. Up to this point, each person perceived and judged the world from the perspective of his or her own currently activated memes. The way the person saw reality was right—not only for that person, but for all the others, too! In the second tier, this changes; we come to a "quantum leap" of the consciousness. From here on out, you are in a position to see that you carry within you all of the previous levels.

Now you can see the whole spiral of your own inner development. You recognize where you stand and where you should perhaps get to. You incorporate, instead of excluding and delimiting. You value each meme as important for the entire spiral of your being. You develop your own worldview and look for the relationships and contexts between all systems and views of the world.

7. *Yellow: integration.* For about fifty years, the idea has existed that life constantly reorganizes itself as a chaotic-creative whole into complex systems. Yellow marks the transition from the industrial society to the society of knowledge. Simplified, "less is more" rep-

resents Yellow values. Information and competence have rank over power, status, possessions, and group interests. The transition to the post-material society is in sight. People prefer flexible work schedules and space to design things their own way. Like the world itself, a love relationship is also seen as a kaleidoscope of natural differences. Rigid roles are avoided, along with noncommitment. Both partners use unconventional methods within open structures to discover which values they want to commit to in their relationship. A high degree of personal responsibility, loyalty, motivation to learn, and willingness to change are desired as binding values. This complexity is fun and often leads the couple to surprisingly simple solutions. *Dualism:* the dualisms of the First Tier are maintained, but are also mastered by learning to live with paradoxes. Our inner contradictions and opposing positions can be unified in a higher third. *Emphasis:* I.

8. *Turquoise: holistic and cosmic consciousness.* The world is an elegantly balanced system of interlocking powers and waves. Everything is connected to everything else in a living interplay, including feelings and knowledge. Global networking and free use of the positive spiral strengths have been apparent for about thirty years. A holistic, intuitive consciousness permeates the image of the couple: the whole universe is a single dynamic organism with its own collective spirit, which also wants to be expressed creatively in the relationship.

Each partner is both independent and part of a larger, empathetic spiritual whole, whose energy and information he or she receives and passes on to the other. In a progressive spiritual attitude, the couple becomes more and more focused on fine nuances and harmonies in the spherical music. The wonderful relationship between material and spirit, the earthly and the godly in each living form is also perceived in one's partner and celebrated. Cooperative-supportive action is understood to be in service of reality, for which both partners motivate each other: What help can we offer the person in our surroundings in the most different memes? In the Turquoise meme, couples prefer a simple, minimalist lifestyle with a maximal inner breadth and generosity. *Emphasis:* We.

9. *Coral.* This meme is not yet describable, but it will certainly appear in our consciousness at some point. We've included it here as a reminder that in each relationship new fields of consciousness can emerge and change your view of the whole. Anticipate it with curious benevolence, in the name of the next generation!

See the Overall Context. The complexity of human consciousness constantly grows because each meme contains all the memes that lie beneath it. When your consciousness is focused on the fifth meme, you have activated the first four memes, and in the best-case scenario they are all still available to you. The sixth meme will open even wider horizons for you. It's important not to undervalue the memes beneath, but to treasure them in all of their own beauty and worth. On each level of consciousness are new forms of appearance, which are absolutely necessary for living together. Despite this, the already achieved fields of consciousness remain living and active in the whole composition of the spiral. This way, this dynamic, vibrant system always provides naturally for ever more complexity.

Discover Your Couple-Memes. Most adults in Western culture move within the Red, Blue, Orange, and Green memes. Your concepts of partnership also stem from various memes. Because they partially contradict each other, they can cause unrest in many relationships.

1. Red wants a spontaneous, self-aware, passionate relationship (in its unhealthy form, violent and invasive).
2. Blue likes a traditional, value-centered, reliable relationship (in its unhealthy form, compulsive and controlling).

3. Orange pleads for a rational or profit-oriented relationship (in its unhealthy form, exploitative and superficial).
4. Green prefers a partnership-like, empathetic, antihierarchical relationship (in its unhealthy form, narcissistic and arbitrary).

Imagine these memes as respectable princes who advise you, the royal couple. Each prince would like the honor of designing your relationship and thinks he has the best concept for it. But your relationship will only remain dynamic in the long term if you as a couple can man-age to combine your trusted princes in the most suitable way. This doesn't mean you have to run through the entire spiral. On the contrary, it is often enough to better appreciate a meme you've neglected to give your relationship new strength. Try to find the healthy kernel of each meme. Within your preferred meme, you can do everything for a loving, affectionate, and fulfilling partnership and thereby contribute to the health of all human relationships.

Let Yourself Be Enchanted by the Jewel Moments. Together you have fantastic opportunities to let the good powers of the consciousness spiral to flow into your relationship. Push yourself to continuously tap into all of the memes. Each healthily lived meme represents a gift for your relationship, and it revitalizes you. Together, they form the crown jewels of a relationship, which constitute the richness of your partnership. Here is a small example of which jewels are to be discovered in the eight memes:

■ Beige: security, protection
■ Purple: magical moments, the magic of togetherness
■ Red: erotic passion, joie de vivre
■ Blue: shared values, loyalty
■ Orange: critical facility, willingness to learn
■ Green: empathy, emotional warmth

- Yellow: the ability to change, paradoxical wisdom
- Turquoise: cooperation, transformation

Simplifying Idea 21:
Reconcile Your Differences

With models like Spiral Dynamics Integral, you gain a new overview for your exploration of the giant adventure land of love. Think of yourself as a pioneer. In our Western culture, we still lack convincing legends of love that can show us mature, profound, engaged, and fulfilling relationships. People didn't used to grow old enough to have such long marriages and to really explore their inner dynamics. It seems that the time is only now ripe for this, and we ourselves with our relationships have been invited to write this new integrative myth.

The Bridge Between the Towers:
The Marriage of Opposites

With your expedition from the tower to the castle, you have shown a very special capability: you can tolerate opposites more easily. The "battle of the sexes" ended for you in the dark forest. What you can still use now is a mutual initiation into what is familiar and precious to the opposite sex. Induct each other, and celebrate the marriage of opposites in your castle! This doesn't cancel out the differences between the sexes. Rather, imagine that waters from two very different rivers flow into a common stream. This creates a new, strong flow that carries both partners and increases the energy between them.

Walk upon the Bridge of Esteem. The bridge between the two towers is the new symbol for your peaceful reconciliation of an inner struggle with the "marriage of opposites." Both sexes wrestle

211

today with the same dilemma; too much fixation on autonomy often leads to a loss in the relationship and a loss of self. Therefore, part of the mature art of partnership is approaching each other over this bridge in a reconciliatory manner.

The Woman's Tower	Bridge	The Man's Tower
traditionally feminine	mature partnership	traditionally masculine
relationship	integration	autonomy
victim	partner	knight
princess	royal couple	hero
indirect	diplomatic	direct
passive	energetic	active
erotic power	creative	productive power
family	community	state
submissive	interactive	dominant
careful	attentive	careless
housework	shared responsibility	gainful employment
caretaking	wealth of functions	provision
women's rights	equality of the sexes	men's rights
intimacy	familiarity	publicity

Create a New Balance. The preceding list invites the both of you to recognize the opposite pole to your own classical gender role. The common living field places the bridge in the middle. You reach it by each going a step toward the opposite pole and integrating aspects of that side into yourself.

Men move in the direction of the "women's pole": relationship, intimacy and submission. Women go in the direction of the "men's pole": autonomy, publicity, dominance. The trick is for both of you to do this at the same time and then to really meet right in the middle, where you find a fair solution. When a woman goes in the direction of the man's tower, she crosses the bridge of

integration. The man, who heads out toward the woman's tower, also spends some time on that bridge. Right in the middle is where integration in your partnership takes place, and there your relationship flourishes gloriously!

Think of Bridge Building as a Project for the Midlife Years. The concept of the "bridge encounters" can make your relationship more complete in the transformative phase of middle age. This time is especially ideal for both men and women. In their mid-fifties, men have a wonderful opportunity to further develop their sensitive and receptive side. They become gentler, more feeling, and more understanding. They feel a great need for a "warm nest" and are ready to become more active within the relationship. So they make a step toward the feminine. (Wise bridge-building men approach their own wives lovingly, not new ones!) For women, these years after the family phase allow them to feel the energy within themselves, to "get going" again. They go out into the world more, wanting to tackle something again, be active in the world  again, and work for spiritual clarity. (Wise bridge-building women attack political and social problems, not their own husbands!)

Open Your Inner Treasure Chamber

If you were able to concentrate all of your attention on what corresponds to your innermost being, you would grasp a wave of enthusiasm. With dancing lightness, you could make your dreams come true. You would leap over walls and work miracles. The treasure chamber of yourself would lay open before you. What could be better than that?

Honor Your Partner as the Midwife of Your True Being. The greatest mistake that people in long-term relationships can make at this point would be to blame their partner for blocking the way to their treasure chamber. Throw this kind of thinking out with the trash, and turn your attitude completely around. Instead, see your partner as the most loyal ally that you have ever had. Your partner is your most loyal companion on the way to your treasure chamber and is the best person to help you finally open yourself again. There is one condition for this, however: you yourself must also be ready to accompany your partner on the path to his or her treasure chamber. This way, you will both become midwives of your true beings, which begins beyond the conventional or collective path.

Ask Eight Liberating Questions. Inspired by Beverly Stewart, an American spiritual trainer, we have put together eight questions for couples. You can use these to break up blockages in your life and bring the true wishes of your heart out of your treasure chamber and into the light.

- *Your heart's magnet.* Where is it pulling you right now? Answer this question intuitively, without thinking, without obligations. That is, avoid thoughts like "Actually, I should feel pulled toward my spouse." Imagine that you are weightless and that a magnet pulls you toward the place, the person, or the activity where your heart would most of all like to be.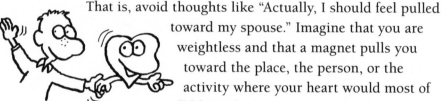

- *Your magical time.* When does time fly by? During which activities can you forget everything around you? What do you always like to do, even on the worst days?

- *Your effortlessness.* What can you do without any strain of will? What do you do that seems to go of its own accord? Which activities are pleasures for you—even when they're challenging? What inspires and fulfills you, even as you are doing it?

- *Your secret thoughts.* Where do your thoughts wander when you let them go? You are usually concentrating on something; you hold your words and ideas within certain boundaries. But for once, when you don't, when you're alone, what do you gravitate toward?

- *Your absorbing tasks.* What can completely engross your attention? When do you forget everything around you? What can you dive into, and where do you feel completely at ease? In what activity do you express your personality best? During what activity are you fully one with yourself?

■ *The location of your dreams.* Where does your soul like to go when you're daydreaming? This can be a real place or a spot that only exists in your fantasies. Almost all people have such a fitting place for themselves inside, to which they can send themselves effortlessly and with lightning speed. What does your place look like?

■ *Your return.* What have you returned to over and over in your life? This can be an activity, a person, an experience, a place, an area of learning, or something else. Again, let your ideas about this question rise up unfiltered. Note them down on a piece of paper, just as they come. Let your pen travel back and forth between these possibilities. Where does your pen (your thoughts) most want to go? After a bit of back and forth, it will get stuck on one point. And that's it!

■ *Your infiniteness.* When money and all professional and family obligations were no object, what would you do with your time? When you find an inner picture here, your heart's wishes climb over the highest obstacle that you have placed for yourself. In this moment, you ignore your usual "Oh, but I couldn't!" and "But not me!" and take a big step in the direction of your life's goal.

Trust the Inspiration of Your Most Loyal Ally. After you have answered all of these questions, it's time to meet with your truest ally. This exchange is like a conspiratorial meeting. The Latin *spirare* means "to create breath," and *spiritus* is "breath, spirit," so *conspirare* means "to breathe together, to breathe with the same spirit." A conspiratorial partner-meeting is thus a "plot for the common good" and an intimate search of two people who want to be in harmony with each other. It's only a small step from conspiring to inspiring!

If you put your answers down next to each other's, you won't find only agreement between them. Some visions even seem to lead away

from your partner. Ask your ally to develop common steps toward your inner vision that give him or her a feeling of strong connection. You should also feel out how you can best support your partner in the realization of his or her vision. Agree to three steps that you can take in the next three weeks to come closer to your goal.

In the Land of Pa(i)radoxical Wisdom

A paradox is a statement that contradicts itself, but also reveals hidden layers of meaning, "Everything is possible, even the impossible!" Paradoxical higher truths exist not only in philosophy, but also in physics, math, astronomy, and statistics. Paradoxes also appear in the wise teachings of great spiritual traditions, in the form of puzzling koans or mystical insights.

Most paradoxes, however, are found in the thoughts and writings about love. The more a person delves into its mysteries, the more contradictory—and believable—statements about love become. As a sign of their deep plunge into love, panorama couples compose their shared reality in paradoxes. We have compiled seven such truths for you:

Because I Never Held You, I Hold You Forever. (Rainer Maria Rilke)
Love has the freedom to not want to possess anyone. Each holds on to the other, but neither holds the other down or holds back the other's

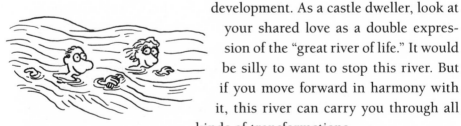

development. As a castle dweller, look at your shared love as a double expression of the "great river of life." It would be silly to want to stop this river. But if you move forward in harmony with it, this river can carry you through all kinds of transformations.

The Best Archer Never Hits the Bulls-Eye. (Zen Koan) Clever head understand that they can't grasp everything about themselves nor about their partner. Arrows that strike in the middle of the heart only hurt and are difficult to pull out. It's enough to scratch your partner slightly in the back with an objection, a criticism, or a wish, because someone who hits exactly in the center is often shooting beyond that target. The optimum is usually something less than everything.

The Heart Also Needs Abundance, Enough Is Never, Ever Enough! (Conrad Ferdinand Meyer) If you are stingy with your love, you are stingy with your own soul. It becomes impoverished and also robs the partner of his or her creative counterpart. A love that freely gives, on the other hand, makes both hearts richer. Don't underestimate the power of small gestures and signs in everyday life. Love takes care of the little things, but it's anything but small-minded. Give away your good wishes, your affection, and your desire for your partner with wasteful joy.

I Am Through You so I. (e. e. cummings) Loving partners become attentive collectors of an infinite number of bits of knowledge about themselves and the other person, which they feed into their shared consciousness. If their shared interpretation is successful, they create a fullness that the I alone could never reach. I owe to my partner the most successful treasure hunt within myself. The desire for loyalty lies in this reliability of inexhaustible searching, knowledge, and interpretation.

If You Disagree with Me, You Have Something to Give Me. (Dom Hélder Câmara) Contradiction is a gift whose acceptance expands your own existence. It allows the unfamiliar to be considered, taken in as an impulse to change, and transformed into your own. Partners in the castle endure contradictions because as men and women they are themselves part of a unity of opposites. Differences of opinion don't divide them. They can also give in without having the feeling that they lose themselves in doing so. On the contrary, they see it as a gain for themselves when the other has gained space.

The Essence of Love Is Something That Neither Shrinks Through Aversion nor Grows Through Affection. (Sufism) Love is attached to the other person, but it is not dependent on his or her reciprocated love. At some point, mature love invites the couple to go beyond themselves and move completely into the realm of love. Then their love no longer belongs to them. They belong to love and become a symbol for it. Love itself loves through them without a specific goal—undemanding, free, and knowing.

Love Is Unending, and with Something Unending, There Is Always Farther to Go. (Blessed Elizabeth of the Trinity) The search for happiness in love is always also a search for meaning in life. Lovers are also searchers for meaning who trust that each person has the ability to advance  into the strange, distant universe through the movements of the heart and the spirit. Love has a cosmic origin, and so it always hopes for unlimited opportunities to unfold. Its ability to expand is boundless. How should love orient itself? In the end, only the immeasurable can be its standard of measurement. Even if a person loves greatly, love itself is always greater than the space the person can fill with his or her love.

Simplifying Idea 22: Live a Royal Love

What does a royal couple do all day? First of all, they live a normal, everyday life, like that of kings and queens. There are lovely pictures of Queen Elizabeth washing dishes in her weekend home. Aside from this, though, royal couples also allow themselves exceptional moments. Here are a few ideas that you can implement, even without a noble title or blue-blooded ancestors.

Five Royal Hours

Happy couples spend more time together than couples who are less happy—that is one of the very clear results of John Gottman's studies observing and interviewing thousands of couples. While he was focusing on the secret recipe of the happy couples, he noticed that they differed from the unhappy ones in the love-time factor. The amount of time spent together wasn't the issue, but rather the quality of time. Here are the five most important kinds of quality time with which you can crown your everyday life together.

- *Time of affection:* Hug, kiss, hold, and touch each other. After a stressful day or an irritating conversation, physical closeness is especially good at calling up emotional closeness. Minimum dose: Five minutes a day.

- *Time of questions:* Grant yourself an audience. This old-fashioned term comes from the Latin word for "to hear," and that's exactly what it's about: ask each other questions and listen as the other answers. Think of clever questions; challenge your partner. This can range from practical plans (e.g., "Where did you always want to take a vacation with me?") to reaching deeper into the soul of the other (e.g., "Are there any wishes left in your heart that I can fulfill for you?"). Calculate about two hours per week for this.

- *Time of recognition:* "She loves me, but she doesn't like me." Men often say this about their wives. Mostly this is a false statement that derives from a genuine human perception; a reproach has more weight than a lot of praise. So you should try to give your partner some praise every day. Don't give sweeping praise (e.g., "You're great"), but rather concrete and honest praise. Express your approval when it comes easily to you. But take time every day to also do it for real. You couldn't give each other a more royal gift. At five minutes a day, this means thirty-five minutes a week.

- *Time of separating:* When one of you leaves the house, say good-bye tenderly and don't rush it. Make sure that you know of at least one event taking place in your partner's life today. Assure the other that you will be thinking of this event— especially if it's something unpleasant. Don't underestimate the bond between your hearts, which this creates. It can be more intense than several cell phone calls. Time required: at least two minutes per good-bye.

■ *Time of greeting:* When you're together again, tell each other about your experiences. Each must tell about something, and each has to be able to listen to the other—even if you're tired or bored. Over the course of time, this lets royal couples develop a culture of witty conversation: during the day, they collect entertaining and touching moments like small precious pearls, which they bring to their partner in the evening. Plan on around twenty minutes per greeting.

■ *Sum: five hours per week:* Presuming that one or both of you leaves the house five days a week, the times given here add up to around five hours per week. That's not even 5 percent of your waking hours. This royal quality time for your relationship can even be managed in times of professional or other kinds of stress. And it bears fruit!

Seven Pieces of Advice for Royal Couples

The great Protestant theologian Jörg Zink and his wife, Heidi, have been together for over sixty years. In a wonderfully written list of maxims, Jörg Zink summarizes the experiences of this long path together to pass it on to younger couples. They contain the great virtues necessary for maturity and highly developed relationships. We are happy to be able to publish them here for the first time:

1. *Give each his own.* Allow your partner his own way, his own time, his own decisions, and his own preferences. Also allow yourself to have shared friends who are important for both of you and who do good for your relationship.

2. *Show each other respect in matters of worldview.* Let the other person go; don't possess her with your ideas. Allow her to have her own thoughts, perceptions, experiences, judgments, and beliefs. You don't always have to know everything about the other per-

son, and she doesn't have to share everything with you, as long as mutual respect reigns between you and nothing has to be denied or hidden.

3. *Be there for each other.* Stay with the other person when his soul is filled with darkness. Stay by him when he is sick or suffering. But give him the freedom to say what he really needs and what he doesn't.

4. *End each night in peace.* No matter what you have just been hammering out, end the estrangement or fight at the end of the day. Don't get stuck on the failures or shortcomings of your partner. Go on in the knowledge that your relationship is greater than the injury it has just experienced. Leave everything behind before the next day.

5. *Adopt each other's visions of the landscape of faith.* Slowly and in small steps, accept the religious experiences of your partner into your own space of belief. Your own decisive experiences don't lose any of their shine. In the end, many of them merge with your partner's into a great river.

6. *Feel each other as close as possible, without analyzing it.* You can never be so close to another person that you know who she is. After many years, she could very well be more than the image that you have of her. Don't pin her to that image!

7. *View each other as a gift.* Don't take it for granted that another person is sharing this life with you. Ask yourself every day what it would be like if you had to live alone. Consider the other person to be a blessing and a gift, even if not all of your dreams are fulfilled. Look at your partner with gratitude, and express it.

The Riddle of Love

Is there a good guiding image for couples that shows freedom and depth in a relationship? While searching for such an image, we came across a couple who are mentioned in the Bible and in sources from the Arabic world: the wise King Solomon and the mysterious Queen of Sheba.

In the folk wisdom of Judaism, Christianity, and Islam are countless legends of a love affair between Solomon and the Queen of Sheba. 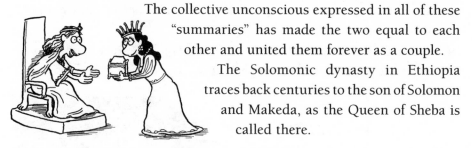 The collective unconscious expressed in all of these "summaries" has made the two equal to each other and united them forever as a couple.

The Solomonic dynasty in Ethiopia traces back centuries to the son of Solomon and Makeda, as the Queen of Sheba is called there.

A Royal Love. Solomon's and Makeda's story became a timeless myth of the interplay of spirit and feeling, richness and generosity, wit and wisdom in love. In the legend in the Old Testament (1 Kings 10:1–13), we have discovered the secret game of love between equals. Let it inspire you to play this game yourself.

- *First move, Makeda:* The rich ruler of Sheba hears of Solomon's riches and wisdom. She travels from far away with a giant caravan full of gifts "to test him with subtle questions. She arrived in Jerusalem with a very numerous retinue, and with camels bearing spices, a large amount of gold, and precious stones. She came to Solomon and questioned him on every subject in which she was interested." What drives the queen is the need of all women for a deep exchange of ideas. She, too, wants to direct the masculine wisdom toward herself and to try it out. For this, she stages a popular parlor game, because women in the Orient could challenge and test a man playfully with tricky riddles.

  Women can win a man by opening new spaces up to him. Offer him "the beautiful interaction with each other" (Friedrich Schiller) by creating a pleasant atmosphere like

Makeda. Choose friendly words as your gift for the host, before you get into the questions on your heart.

If your wife confronts you with a difficult question, don't see this as an attack or harassment, but rather as the opening move of a game of riddles. Show yourself as her equal by solving the relationship riddle posed by her. She won't be content with throwaway answers. She wants to know  what is deep inside of you, if you can feel your way into her and the relationship, and what she can admire in you.

■ *Second move, Solomon:* "King Solomon explained everything she asked about, and there remained nothing hidden from him that he could not explain to her." The king takes Makeda seriously and addresses all of her questions.

The art of this move consists in the man not standing there with blank cards. You have to know beforehand which questions could come. The more you have thought about your relationship and have empathized with your wife, the more easily you can answer her questions.

As a wife, you should ask questions and not present conditions or challenges. Give your husband the chance to find his own answer to your questions. Like the queen, rely on his competence, his understanding of the subject matter, and his judgment, which he shows in his profession. Trust him to give you his best.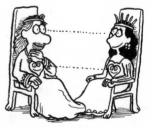

■ *Third move, Makeda:* "But as the Queen of Sheba witnessed Solomon's great wisdom, the palace he had built, the food at his table, the seating of his ministers, the attendance and garb of his waiters, his banquet service and the sacrifices he offered in the temple of the Lord, she was breathless. 'The report I heard in my country about your deeds and your wisdom is true,' she told the king. 'Though I did not believe the report until I came and saw with my own eyes, I have discovered that they were not telling me the half. Your wisdom and prosperity surpass the report I heard.'" The queen is enraptured and showers Solomon with gifts. The questioning was worthwhile; this man had shown depth and intuition.

When a wife experiences this kind of wonderful moment of fullness with her partner, she should show her husband her honest, unqualified admiration and her respect. Grant him this confirmation, and tell him how unique he is.

Like Solomon, a husband should make sure that the wealth of his "secular home" is always outdone by the beauty of his "inner heart's temple." Solomon knew that the organ of the mind is a listening, empathetic heart. This is where your wisdom comes from!

- *Fourth move, Solomon:* "King Solomon gave the queen of Sheba everything she desired and asked for, besides such presents as were given her from Solomon's royal bounty." Now the king also has fun with the win-win relationship game. His passion is awakened. Like any enthusiastic man, he grows beyond himself. He easily fulfills all of the queen's wishes and discovers that he can still give much more of himself.

A husband should engage in this positive competition in love. The heart of each relationship is the relationship of hearts. Start now with the game of riddles yourself. You'll be amazed at what riches are slumbering inside the two of you and what fullness will become visible in your relationship.

As a wife, you should be receptive to his attempts at inner reflection. Meet him halfway (the smart queen went much further!). The more heartfelt warmth you give out, the more shared win-win experiences are possible between you.

■ *Fifth move, both players:* "Then she returned with her servants to her own country." This last move allows the two of you to also have your own empire within the relationship. Each can stand for him- or herself, just as the two towers of your individuality in the center of your castle stand for you. A healthy autonomy doesn't destroy the bridge of connection between the two of you, but rather supports it. Admit to each other that you are unique individuals. Allow each other to always go back to your "own land." Show the freedom of your love with the sentence, "You are valuable to me in that which you do for yourself."

A Game Theory for Lovers. Solomon and Makeda ask the same questions as all lovers. Who am I? Who are you really? Is the inner realm of your soul also as beautiful as you are on the outside? Both of you make sure that there can be no losers in the game of love. With this, you have anticipated an insight from modern game theory, which says that there are only three possible outcomes of a game:

■ *The lose-lose solution.* Both partners play so that each asks too much or gives too little. Consequently, both lose. In love, such a game means the end. The relationship fails because of excessive demands.

■ *The win-lose solution.* Here there is a winner and a loser. One must always tend to the balance. The winner must be able to be the loser the next time, and vice versa. This variant can work, but it also can quickly make your love into a constant tallying project, where you're always calculating who's ahead. In the worst-case scenario, you monitor each other and start to suspect that you're always paying each other back for your mistakes.

■ *The win-win solution*. Both are winners. You can't lose anymore, because your partner makes sure that you profit and always maintain a good position. Unimaginative strategies don't work here. Paradoxical, contradictory, puzzling, and playful ideas, on the other hand, bring success—and guarantee your future. Because more excitement, interest, and hope of happiness develop, this solution is a favorite in the history of evolution.

Alternating Attentiveness, Immediate Reaction. Solomon and Makeda set their sights on just this kind of win-win solution of mutual gain. They finely tune their moves to each other. As soon as one asks something, wants something, gives something, or does something, the other moves immediately and continues the game. They alternate making their moves; the excitement for the opposition and the expectant anticipation of the next move are always maintained. Thus a sensual process is set in motion between the two of them.

The Magnificence of Kings: Empathy and Understanding. You also master the king's magnificent art in the game of riddles of love as soon as you combine the two most important powers of love intelligently: first, the power of empathizing with the other person, and second, the power to truly understand the other.

■ *You can learn the gift of empathy*. Solomon owed his wisdom to an early insight: He had understood that he (like many other men) needed to develop more emotional competence to reach real maturity. So as a young man, he asked God for a listening, understanding heart (1 Kings 3). Without inner warmth and a lively sensitive ability, people "petrify" in their later years: their faces become stiff and stubborn, their feelings become bitter or die off, and their whole attitude becomes egocentric. A hearing, empathetic heart, on the other hand, stays young and lively.

You reach real empathy through questions like, "What has hurt you?" "What do you need?" "What are you suffering from?" "How can I comfort you?" "What will ease your pain?"

Ask these questions with a loving look not only at your partner, but also at your own heart.

- *You can also seek the gift of understanding.* This may not be as strenuous as Makeda's long journey through the desert to Solomon. If you carefully and patiently think over yourself, your partner, and your relationship, your own prejudices or limitations will become clear. New contexts appear, and the interpretation of your experiences gains depth.

  You can achieve more insight through the following questions: "What have I not yet seen, considered, or understood with respect to my partner or myself?" "What is his behavior trying to show me, beyond the obvious?" "What is the deeper meaning of this situation?" "What higher wisdom could be hiding behind it for us?"

- *Unite empathy and understanding into wisdom.* Empathy and understanding give you access to "all the treasures of this world." Now you receive the greatest gift of your love, which you have served so long and so loyally: the hidden image of life appears. The overall scene is revealed to the two of you, the "view" of the great state of being. Up until now, the beating heart of your relationship has led you. Now you have found your new center in the heart of life. The Biblical word for this knowing devotion to what is greater than oneself is wisdom.

Resources

The First Dwelling of Love: The Tower

Martha Beck, *Finding Your Own North Star: Claiming the Life You Were Meant to Live.* New York: Three Rivers Press, 2002; and *The Joy Diet: 10 Daily Practices for a Happier Life.* New York: Crown, 2003. Simply worth reading and following, with many practical exercises.

Clarissa Pinkola Estés, *Women Who Run with the Wolves: Myths and Stories of the Wild Woman Archetype.* New York: Ballantine Books, 1996. We found the list of the stages of life in this women's best-seller by a depth psychologist and trauma therapist. A must-have for anyone who likes C. G. Jung and the interpretation of fairy tales.

Gay Hendricks, *Conscious Living: Finding Joy in the Real World.* New York: Harper San Francisco, 2000. The second part of this book illustrates particularly well the fact that love is built upon self-respect and self-discipline.

Tiki Küstenmacher and Lothar J. Seiwert. *How to Simplify Your Life: Seven Practical Steps to Letting Go of Your Burdens and Living a Happier Life.* New York: McGraw-Hill, 2004. Here you'll find countless practical tips that make your everyday life together easier: cleaning out your closets, organizing, handling your finances, and so on.

Eva-Maria Zurhorst, *Love Yourself, and It Doesn't Matter Who You Marry!* Carlsbad, Calif.: Hay House, 2007. A top seller about how marriage can become a site of inner healing.

The Second Dwelling of Love: The Love Tent

Joseph Campbell, *The Power of Myth*. New York: Anchor, 1991. We thank the chapter "Tales of Love and Marriage" for the idea of the three stars of love: Eros, Agape, and Amor.

Gay and Kathlyn Hendricks, *Conscious Loving: The Journey to Co-Commitment: A Way to Be Fully Together Without Giving Up Yourself*. New York: Bantam, 1990. Contains a sensible training program for co-engagement in a relationship.

Jack Morin, *The Erotic Mind: Unlocking the Inner Sources of Passion and Fulfillment*. New York: HarperCollins, 1995. Here we found the ten rules of the game of erotic communication.

Haruki Murakami, *South of the Border, West of the Sun: A Novel*. New York: Vintage, 2000. The ideas from Murakami that we used come from an interview he gave in the German magazine *Brigitte*.

The Third Dwelling of Love: The Homestead

Steve Biddulph, *Manhood: An Action Plan for Changing Men's Lives*. Lane Cove, New South Wales, Australia: Finch Publishing, 1995. Excellent tips for how men can regain and pass on good paternal energy.

John M. Gottman and Nan Silver, *The Seven Principles for Making Marriage Work*. New York: Crown, 1999. All books by John Gottman are recommended all-around.

John Gray, *Men Are from Mars, Women Are from Venus: A Practical Guide for Improving Communication and Getting What You Want in Your*

Relationships. New York: HarperCollins, 1993; *Mars and Venus in the Bedroom: A Guide to Lasting Romance and Passion*. New York: HarperCollins, 1995; *Men Are from Mars, Women Are from Venus Book of Days: 365 Inspirations to Enrich Your Relationships*. New York: HarperCollins, 1998. Gray's popular therapy concept stems from the acceptance of the differences between men and women. Sometimes a bit schematic, as the qualities they share are at least as interesting as their differences.

Patty Howell and Ralph Jones, *World Class Marriage: How to Create the Relationship You Always Wanted with the Partner You Already Have*. Valley Village, Calif.: HJ Books, 2002. Sixteen ground rules for a good relationship.

Carl Gustav Jung, *Collected Works of C. G. Jung*. Princeton: Princeton University Press, 2000. You will find Jung's concept of the simple partner and the complicated partner in the section titled "Marriage as a Psychological Relationship."

Pepper Schwartz, *Peer Marriage: How Love Between Equals Really Works*. New York: Free Press, 1994. On the deep friendship of equal partnerships and the social obstacles that must be overcome to achieve them.

Ken Wilber, *Integral Psychology: Consciousness, Spirit, Psychology, Therapy*. Boston: Shambhala, 2000. Wilber's "Levels of Nourishment" name the basic needs of interpersonal relationships and inspired our five-field system.

The Fourth Dwelling of Love: The Dark Forest

On the dragon typology: the nine dragons come from the personality models of the enneagrams. You will find an introduction to this system at the end of our book *How to Simplify Your Life*.

Andreas Ebert and Richard Rohr, *Discovering the Enneagram: An Ancient Tool for a New Spiritual Journey*. New York: HarperCollins,

1991. The spiritual bestseller on the topic, written very practically and with humor.

John Gottman, *Why Marriages Succeed or Fail: And How You Can Make Yours Last.* New York: Simon and Schuster, 1994. The four horsemen of the apocalypse are shown here in detail and are effectively battled. Very worthwhile.

Rosemarie Welter-Enderlin, *Deine Liebe ist Nicht Meine Liebe.* Freiburg, Germany: Herder, 2000. We have learned much from this book. An excellent foundational work for systemic family and couples therapy with a clear look at social processes that act upon relationships. It is not available in English.

The Fifth Dwelling of Love: The Castle

Don Edward Beck and Christopher C. Cowan, *Spiral Dynamics: Mastering Values, Leadership, and Change.* Williston, Vt.: Blackwell Publishing, 1996.

Hans Jellouschek, *Die Kunst als Paar zu Leben.* Stuttgart, Germany: Kreuz, 2005. A "good inner couples' image" makes this book reader-friendly, practical, and wise. It is not available in English.

Aaron Kipnis and Elizabeth Herron, *Gender War, Gender Peace: The Quest for Love and Justice Between Women and Men.* New York: William Morrow and Company, Inc., 1994. This exciting book inspired our bridge-building between the two towers of man and woman.

Ken Wilber, *A Brief History of Everything.* Boston: Shambhala, 2001. Our greatest task is to realize our spirituality through careful, empathetic service in culture, nature, and society. Sophisticated reading on the current consciousness debates of the postmodern era.

Index

Index

Index

Index